A LITTLE COLLECTION OF SHORT STORIES

A JOURNEY FROM MONTMARTRE TO YORKSHIRE VIA NEW YORK AND HIROSHIMA

First Published in Great Britain 2019 by Mirador Publishing

Copyright © 2019 by Michael Haley

All rights reserved. No part of this publication may be reproduced or transmitted, in any form or by any means, without permission of the publishers or author. Excepting brief quotes used in reviews.

First edition: 2019

Any reference to real names and places are purely fictional and are constructs of the author. Any offence the references produce is unintentional and in no way reflects the reality of any locations or people involved.

A copy of this work is available through the British Library.

ISBN: 978-1-913264-17-8

Mirador Publishing
10 Greenbrook Terrace
Taunton
Somerset
UK
TA1 1UT

A little Collection of short Stories

*A journey from
Montmartre to Yorkshire
via
New York and Hiroshima*

Michael Haley

Introduction

In this selection of writings you will find not only short stories but also poems or song lyrics that tell a story. Some of them are my personal experiences or recollections. Some are rants about things I may have felt strongly about at some time. Some are cliff hangers and some are extracted chapters from my previous novels.

The collection has been assembled here in random order. Although I have subtitled this collection "A journey from Montmartre to Yorkshire via New York and Hiroshima.", from a geographical point of view, along the way I also visit Auschwitz, Charleston in South Carolina, Maldon, Stansted Airport and Blairgowrie in Scotland.

Furthermore, from a chronological point of view, my visits include the 30's, the 50's, the 60's, two World Wars, the 10th and 15th centuries, , the present, the past, and real and imagined futures.

Please feel free to laugh, cry, smile or sigh; to be amused, delighted, disturbed or horrified. You are not, I hope, permitted to be bored.

Most of all, enjoy!

A Small Collection of Short Stories

Montmartre Steps 1938	24th November, 2011
Obsession	4th March, 2015
Elm Park Ragamuffin Boy	28th September, 2012
(The magic, the madness and the mystery)	
Clock of the Seasons	2nd January, 2003
The Nature of Reality	21st July, 2014
Cardiac Arrest	June 1996
(A talking blues)	
The Way I am Now	7th August, 2018
Lost Child	8th January, 2006
Angel's Holiday	3rd December, 2012
Little Red Riding Hood	15th February, 2015
(rewritten for 2015)	
Punk Piece - Another Turn of the Screw	5th/7th August, 2012
Confusion	10th October, 2017
Gridlocked	29th December, 2017
Wednesday at the Wine Bar	25th to 27th April 2012
The Merryweather	23rd March, 2015
Swinging Sixties	21st December, 2011 to 4th January, 2012
(A Talking Blues)	
Upside Down	4th January, 2013
Opportunity too good to miss	31st January, 2015
(Originally "A star in my pocket")	
Henry's Operation	13th July, 2015
Auction	17th to 22nd November, 2015
(If Things Don't Change)	

A Change from the Norm	24th to 27th February 2012
(Originally "A few days in the life of a man with a Porsche")	
The Man in Dark Glasses	22nd October, 2015
Clever Clive and the Mushroom Harvest - The Full Story	Sometime during 1993/4, and in February 2014
Maldon, 11th August, 991	27th April, 2018
(1027 years after the battle. Well, better late, than never!)	
The Nutivity 2014	24th to 27th November, 2014
(A gherkin birth)	
The eyes follow you around the room	20th to 27th January, 2014
(Originally "The Painting")	
Remember Road	22nd November, 2011
Have you seen the latest newscast?	6th May, 2015
Don't Talk to Me about Gherkins	12th July, 2016
Diversions	15th September, 2014
Thank You. No!	1st June, 2014
Angel's Mission	24th December, 2014 to 5th January, 2015
Courgette	21st October, 2014
(The story of Cheryl and Pete)	
The Guitarist	9th April, 2015
And the band played on	16th/28th March, 2014
The Man who sold the World	1st/4th February, 2016
Dangerous Curves	5th to 10th April, 2012
Luftwaffe Reprise	Tuesday 8th May 2012
Westward Ho! Ho! Ho!	
(Originally a script for a short play, 19th October, 2014)	
(Rewritten as a story 30th December 2014 to 6th January 2015)	
Oh Happy Day?	21st October 2016
Zebra in t' Chippie	17th to 19th November, 2016

Montmartre Steps 1938
(Written 24th November, 2011)

I am a streetlamp, standing tall and proud in the middle of a beautiful cascade of steps in the urban village of Montmartre in Paris. I am slim, black and very elegant, and I love my job, keeping the streets illuminated and safe for people to walk at night. Together with the other streetlamps I have stood sentry over these steps for over a hundred years, and I can remember when we were originally powered by smelly gas. Now it's nice clean electricity. At my age I might get a bit rusty and corroded through the winter, and so once a year, the Monsieur comes along and gives me and my colleagues a nice new coat of shiny black paint.

It's not a problem standing still all the time, and we see lots of interesting people go by, but the trees standing on the steps with us do seem to have a better life and more fun.

In the winter, they are just like us streetlamps, bare, cold and dark, but even then they seem to dance in the wind. In spring they grow new branches, leaves and blossom, as they burst into life with the warmer weather, and then they smell so sweet and lovely, in their luscious green for the summer. Birds perch in their branches, and sing. People shelter under their boughs in the summer rain. Lovers stop and kiss in their shady refuge.

Ah, but best of all, they are so magnificent in the autumn, as their leaves turn a myriad of shades of brown, red, gold and yellow, before the winds come and blow the leaves to the bottom of the steps, for the Monsieur to sweep up. I know us lamps are smart and bright, but we remain aloof and detached, while the trees are alive, and always changing.

Oh, I wish I was a tree!

But now it seems there's more than that to worry about. I've seen the planes in the skies above us, and I've eavesdropped on the conversations of people talking as they pass up and down the steps. They say that there's going to another war, and that the planes will drop bombs on our beautiful streets. The music in the cafes and bars nearby will stop playing, and we will be chopped down and taken away, to be melted down and made into weapons and ammunition.

Oh, I wish I was a tree!

Obsession
(Written 4th March, 2015)

Colin was limping round the builder's yard on his walking stick when his mobile phone rang.

"We've got problems at the Ingatestone site, Boss. The Polish boys have downed tools again."

"What's up now? Has that arsehole Cousins been stirring them up?"

"I don't know, Boss. Their gangmeister Wazilevski says they're not laying another brick until you pay them what you owe in back wages; says that they've got rent to pay and wives and kids to keep fed and watered."

Eddie was used to mopping up little disputes for the boss. As Colin's right hand man he'd been in the business long enough to know how the men at the coalface worked and thought. But this was different.

Something sinister was going on. Not a week went by without further niggles on the Ingatestone job, and Eddie was growing tired of having barrow loads of shit thrown at him. Colin had problems of his own. In the past 2 weeks his company had lost a lucrative rolling contract with Wagstaffe's for the buildings maintenance of a large spread of properties owned by a local housing association. This had been the bread and butter contract that kept CJ Builders ticking over, and now it was gone, and it was pretty obvious who had stolen it.

The telephone tension intensified

"I know what's going on," screamed Colin, "I bet you a pound to a pinch of snuff that fucking Ryan fucking Cousins is behind this. He just keeps boiling the broth. I'm going round to see him right now."

"Not a good idea, Boss," Eddie replied calmly, "We need to get the boys back to work quickly. We've got deadlines to meet on this job, and we're a week behind already. It won't do any good at all to ruffle Cousin's feathers.

You and I know that sooner or later he will get his comeuppance, and all we need to do is make sure that we're there to pick up the pieces and laugh in his face. One day he'll trip over his size 12 work boots and we will have the opportunity to nick all the work back that he has stolen from us."

There was a pause and a sigh as Colin's short fuse was temporarily snuffed.

"You're right as usual," Colin agreed, "I'll sort out that little shit heap later. In the meantime what do you think we should do?"

"Well! The Polaks insist on seeing you; so you need to get down here quick, and come with some hard cash, or we'll be up to our armpits in it for certain."

Eddie usually kept the lid on things with a calm approach and he wanted to make sure of an easy outcome, so he added, "Oh! And listen, Boss."

"Yes, mate. What!"

"Take a happy pill on the way here and don't turn up all guns blazing or I'm pretty sure they'll wreck the place and walk away."

"I'm at the yard in Hatfield Peveril right now. Be with you in 20 minutes. OK?"

The chilly April rains always played havoc with Colin's left leg, and as he limped across the yard towards his dark blue van a foreboding cloud hung over him. The extraordinary combination of metal plates, pins and bones holding his leg together enabled him to be mobile, but the downside was the draining discomforting distress in his limited movement which forced him to take painkillers every day. Furthermore, he could never get away from the fact that the underlying cause of this disability had been the impatience of the man he had once known as a true friend and business partner. For a long time, ever since the "accident", Ryan Cousins had been the bane of his life.

Wazilevski sat on low wall together with his little gang. They were all drinking strong sweet coffee from a large thermos flask and smoking skinny roll-your-own cigarettes as they chatted quietly in their native Polish. Their faces showed strain and tension, just as the tone of their conversation and their mannerisms illustrated despair and depression. "Waz" was the spokesman; the man who had a competent command of the English language and looked after the other 3 men. Colin approached him and he stood up and as was customary he shook the gangmeister's hand.

The Boss smiled uneasily, "Good morning gentlemen. What's the problem?"

"Mr Johnson; we have not been paid for 3 weeks. We have no money to pay bills, buy food and get to work. Please! We want to work, but we can't do that for nothing."

Waz smiled. His plea was polite and condescending. Eddie looked at Colin, but both remained silent.

"We are good workers; don't want trouble, but you must pay or we will walk away."

The Boss's fuse was relit and his sidekick saw the blue touch paper about to burst into flames. Colin was absolutely convinced that his arch enemy, Ryan Cousins, was at the bottom of this.

Eddie diverted attention, "OK, Waz, give us a minute would you?" he said with a smile, leading his boss away a few yards.

Quietly he asserted, "There is no way out if you want to have any chance of meeting the deadlines. Pay up or we'll be bollixed. It's the only way, Boss."

Shoulders shrugged in mutual understanding and they stared at each other eye to eye. They both knew that they were trapped.

"OK!" said Colin reluctantly, taking a large wodge of notes out of his inside jacket pocket.

Boss, sidekick and gangmeister stood in a circle and quiet mumbles about amounts of back pay finalised with the passing over of a bundle of cash.

Colin couldn't resist asserting his status as the other Polish boys smiled at their victory by instructing them, "Now get back to work or I'll have you all deported back to your little tin pot third world country."

"We need to talk, mate," the under pressure head man said to his foreman, "Get in the van."

They drove to the Red Lion in Margaretting not saying much to each other. Two pints of bitter weren't going to solve the dilemma, but would serve to loosen tongues a little.

"We can't put up with any more delays on this job. We are already at least 2 days behind because of the recent bad weather, and if the late completion penalties come into play we'll be working for peanuts. After losing the Wagstaffe contract we are totally dependent on this job coming in on time, otherwise I have to seriously consider our future options, which might include declaring bankruptcy."

"OK, Boss, I understand. So what do you want me to do?"

"Crack the whip! Keep them bloody foreigners in line; pray we don't have any more rain; and get the job finished on schedule."

"I'll do my best, Boss."

"I know I can depend on you, Eddie, but the situation is becoming all too much for me. My fucking leg hurts so much in this damp weather, the company's in danger of going tits up, and Vivian's operations are costing me a king's ransom."

"How is Vivian at the moment?"

"She's OK; been over in the States for the latest operation, and I've no idea at the moment when she'll be back; soon I hope."

Two more pints were ordered and the subject of conversation shifted.

Eddie quaffed a large bitter fix and looked his boss straight in the eyes.

"Right!" he said, "As far as Ryan Cousins is concerned, I think it's best if we just ignore getting even until the Ingatestone job is done."

"I can't wait to undermine that little shit faced cheat. Every job we tender for we lose to him because he's got the council's planning department wined and dined, the building regulations boys in his pocket, and the local casual workforce running scared if they don't doff their caps to him. We were just lucky to get this job, and now he wants to screw it up for us."

"Yes, I know, Boss. Let's not panic. Like I say, the time will come for us to get even."

After a while the two men finished their drinks, and the blue van returned to the building site, where Eddie began cracking the whip and praying for fine weather as requested. Colin drove back to the yard and spent the rest of the day going through his contacts book trying to drum up some more work. All he managed to get for his efforts were 3 days work for one man during the following week.

Just before he left the yard a thin brown envelope popped through the letter flap in the porta-cabin. Colin opened it almost knowing what it would say before he read it. It was from Caine and Turner, a local developer.

"Dear Sir,

We are sorry to advise you that on this occasion you have been unsuccessful in bidding for the work to construct a block of 10 apartments on the Chelmer

Basin project. We are most grateful for your interest in tendering and hope that we will be able to do business with you in the future.

Yours faithfully,
Bernard E. Caine - Developments Director"

"Oh, that just takes the biscuit," the despairing builder angrily told himself, "And don't tell me. I know for sure who got the contract instead of me. It was fucking Ryan fucking Cousins again."

Later that evening he felt very sorry for himself. He never slept very well in the double bed on his own without Vivian to keep him warm. He took 2 paracetamol and washed them down with a large tumbler of Bushmills.

Colin was supervising a delivery of 5 pallets of bricks and 4 of them had been put in position with perfect precision. The skies were dark and angry and icy rain was lashing down. The forklift truck carrying the 5th pallet came towards him with what appeared to be breakneck speed, and he shouted "Stop! Stop!" as he edged backwards noticing that the pile of bricks had become unstable and began to tilt towards him. Then he tumbled full length on his back into some footings still shouting, but the forklift continued on course straight at him. As the pile began to topple over he felt each brick hit him like a prize heavyweight boxer was throwing a succession of punches to his body. He screamed as he felt the crunch of bones and 5 of his ribs breaking in slow motion as the brick stack tumbled. Ryan Cousins was driving the forklift and he was laughing as if he were being told a series of one-liner jokes at the Comedy Club as each brick crunched into the helpless builder's body. The slow motion agony continued as the main bulk of the bricks fell in a unified heap on the victim's left leg smashing bones and trapping him underneath.

He shrieked, "It's killing me! It's killing me! It's killing......"

Then he woke up, drenched in sweat, breathless; his heart pounding like a kettle drum; his arms thrashing from side to side desperately chucking off imaginary bricks. He felt like his ribs had been pounded to brick dust and his left leg was throbbing in excruciating pulses of sheer torture. This was the nightmare that he had endured dozens of times before; the one where Ryan Cousins just sat on the forklift grinning at him with unadulterated pleasure while he suffered death by a thousand bricks.

Worse still he knew what would happen now, just as it had so many times before. Now he would lay awake for hours replaying events in his mind just as if he were watching a film on in-demand TV. All of the scenes that led up to the accident would be cruelly laid before him. He would see Ryan and himself being the best of friends, setting up a construction and building business together and having great success in their business and personal lives. They would holiday together with their partners in Balearic and Greek island hotspots like Ibiza and Rhodes. Colin would be with Vivian and Ryan with Simone. Mutual friends would regard the foursome as inseparable. That was the happy bit of the tale.

In the follow on of this waking nightmare Colin's brain would then illustrate the acrimonious break up of the company and then reel off every contract the 2 men had competed for. He would see that ever since the accident he had been embroiled in a mutual vendetta against his former colleague Ryan, and how this had become an all oh so prominent in his business life.

But this time the harrowing thought processes would end differently.

Before exhaustion and the need for comfortable sleep took him away from the vision he found himself saying, "This can't go on. I've had enough. Cousins must die. Cousins must die. Cousins must die."

He fell into a deep sleep with one coherent thought on his mind that stayed with him and would be his first brain reflex of the morning. The situation was no longer merely a competitive vendetta. Now it was an obsession, and Colin was intent on hatching a plan to kill his adversary and take back everything that he considered to be rightfully his property.

He told himself, "Ryan Cousins days are numbered. He is going to be ground into the dirt. I'm going to wipe him clean off the planet."

Elm Park Raggamuffin Boy
(The magic, the madness and the mystery)
(Written 28th September, 2012)

Despite the name there were no trees in Ennerdale Avenue, but there were neat front gardens, and privet hedges and number 36 had its own front door, painted red, and a back garden, and an outside toilet. The war was long over, at least to a child four years is a long time, and the world crept slowly out of its devastation like a snail slides determined across the pavement. The country was on its knees, unable to make ends meet without the most desperate of measures, but the people had already proved to be indomitable, and they were not about to be undermined by rationing, shortages and deprivation. Nobody could have dared to declare that it was the best of times, but clearly it couldn't be the worst of times either.

And in the midst of his safe haven,
In a world of desolation,
Lived a ruffian, a raggamuffin boy,
A waif of a child, skinny, pale, undernourished, naive.
He wore a snotty nose with pride,
His hand me down, jumble sale clothes could not be denied,
His shoes were 2 sizes too big, his laces untied,
He was standing bedraggled in the freezing rain, and never, ever easily cried,
In a house where the cupboard was guarded by old mother Hubbard, Yes!
Always bare!
Austerity the daily norm, poverty the regime everywhere,
No shelter from the storm, careworn and forlorn,
He wandered puzzled down his homebound lanes, beneath the heavy skies.

    Sometimes the longest summer arrived, and the summer rains were warm, and if there were thunder storms, he would hide under the table just as if it were an air raid. He learned to protect himself from the lightning by not holding metal things like knives, and by counting the time between lightning and thunder to know how far away the storm was.

He walked to school, come rain or shine, and walking in the fog was fun.

And when the winter snows fell he played outside with everyone, wearing a hand-knitted bobble hat, and fingerless gloves.

His shoes let the water in until his toes were frozen like icicles, and then the snowman building and snowball fighting had to stop. Then, he'd go indoors to a coal fire, smelly, smoky, dirty, but always welcoming, and warm his toes on the hearth until they were fully thawed. Sundays were the favourite days, a weekly bath after the Sunday roast, and a hot water bottle for a nice warm bed.

In the early years at the Dunningford School, he quickly learned the teacher's rules,

Got the slipper and the cane, broke the rules, felt the pain.

He hated school dinners, especially the everyday mashed potato and stewed cabbage, learned all his times tables, and discovered that all the girls were pretty except for Eileen Brown. But then he and she were the two smelliest, dirtiest, scruffiest kids in the school, and so the teacher always put them together for the last lesson on Fridays, which was country dancing. Worse still, at playtime Eileen always wanted to play kiss chase.

The child learned words and rhymes and useful phrases like:

Liar, liar, your pants are on fire, and

Sticks and stones may break my bones, but names will never hurt me.

And then there was;

Three dirty birds, sitting on the kerbs,

Chirpin' and a burpin' and eatin' dirty worms.

Or:

Spring has sprung, the grass has riz,

I wonder where the birdies is,

Some people say the bird is on the wing, but that's absurd,

The wing is on the bird.

Times were hard, and the latch key kid went home to an empty house, and pulled the key on a string through the letterbox to let himself in. He made himself tea and toast, because his Mum was working at the factory, and his Dad had disappeared.

Often at 5:30 he strolled the 100yards to the bus stop in Rosewood Avenue, an avenue with trees, to meet his Mum off the 165 bus. The raggamuffin boy greeted her with a white mouse in his pocket, and an alarm clock to tell the time in his hand. The first question was "What's for tea?" Whatever it was, it was basic, inventive and filling, and given with the good advice of "Eat it all up, because that's all there is!"

At least Friday's were different, it was payday, and there was fish and chips, and if he was lucky the luxury of a banana or a small bar of chocolate. His dreams were punctuated with foody thoughts of R. Whites lemonade, Smith's crisps (with the little blue bag of salt), Jubblies and Old English Spangles.

And so, his apprenticeship was served with grazing knees, falling out of trees whilst scrumping, or collecting conkers, and often spending all day in the park with Jimmy Saywood and Michael Broad playing football or cricket or just annoying the girls.

He wasn't always alone in the house, but with a permanent absentee dad he was the only boy among 5 girls, including mum, big sisters, who were 8 and 10 years older, and little sisters who were 2 and 3 years younger.

In the raggamuffin boy's world people had names and jobs to do. There was the coalman, the milkman, the bread van, the rag and bone man, and the mobile shop that sold everything. They were all happy, good people.

Then, there was the rent man, a grumpy, bad man, and when he came you had to go and hide, and pretend there was nobody home.

It was a time of simple pleasures, games played with paper, sticks, and stones. Sometimes just flying a kite made from bamboo canes, brown paper, sticky tape and string. Then there were other more dodgy pursuits like scrumping, pulling up potatoes or rhubarb from the nearby farmer's fields, knock down ginger, penny for the guy, and bob a job week (even though he wasn't in the scouts). And there were simple games like snakes and ladders, ludo, jacks, fivestones, hopscotch, and watching the girls play with skipping ropes. He loved going to his Nanna's house in Rainham all by himself on the bus, and especially eating a bag of chips on the top deck of the bus on the way home, feeling very grown up and a bit scared at the same time.

To have a ride in a car was exciting, and to ride in Uncle Ronnie's timber lorry was even better.

The big sisters liked the new music played on their gramophone. Rock and roll was the new Rock and roll. Elvis was stuck somewhere called Heartbreak Hotel and then went to jail but still sang about it. Somebody pleaded not to step on his blue suede shoes, somebody else found his thrill on Blueberry Hill, and yet another fellow told him "Be bopa lula she's my baby".

Yes, the raggamuffin boy's days were filled with fun and adventure, the years were like millennia, and there was always a magic in the air. Not least of all when a brief glimpse of plenty was fuelled by the magic of believing in Father Christmas.

Dotted amongst the magic there was a world of madness where all at once everything seemed to be inside out, upside down, and back to front, and everybody just muddled along from day to day.

Through it all, hope was sustained by the mystery of all the wonderful experiences that lay ahead in the life of a raggamuffin boy.

That boy was me, and still is. No longer smelly and dirty, I hope! And also not so naive!

Many, many years later, in a very different world, and armed with all the priceless wealth of experience, the magic still endures, the madness still perplexes, and the mystery still continues to fascinate.

Clock of the Seasons
(Written 2nd January, 2003)

Round and around, round and around,
the clock of the seasons goes round and around.
So praise be to He who holds the gold key
in the stock of the lock for the spring to be wound.
So praise be to He, forever to see
the clock of the seasons goes round and around.
Round and around, round and around;
the clock of the seasons goes round and around.

In a cold, pale, low sky, a gold watery sun
slow rises to say a new day's just begun,
and cruel deep winds blow, and high-heaped snows fall;
while the white Christmas Winter is the hope for us all,
and eerie thin shadows scratch their names on the ground,
as the clock of the seasons goes round and around.
Round and around, round and around;
the clock of the seasons goes round and around,

Wild cherry blossoms as morning birds sing
a warm, welcome song to our fair maiden of Spring.
She spins and she weaves sweet new grass and green leaves,
as a carpet of bluebells sweeps under the trees,
and all God's small creatures awake safe and sound,
as the clock of the seasons goes round and around.
Round and around, round and around;
the clock of the seasons goes round and around,

When a fire-flame red sky, 'ere fall of warm night
paints Heaven's blue yonder for our shepherd's delight,
and butterflies flutter, and bumble bees hover,
in the shade of a willow by a lazy green river,
and Summertime rides her long merry-go-round,
as the clock of the seasons goes round and around.
Round and around, round and around;
the clock of the seasons goes round and around,

Now mellow fruits ripen down blackberry lanes.
Summer bids us farewell for strong winds and sharp rains.
Wild harvest moon horses under shooting stars dance,
and fairies cast circles in the damp, dewy grass,
and reds, golds, and yellows now shower the ground
as the clock of the seasons goes round and around.
Round and around, round and around;
the clock of the seasons goes round and around.

Round and around, round and around,
The clock of the seasons goes round and around.
So praise be to He, who holds the gold key
in the stock of the lock for the spring to be wound.
So praise be to He, forever to see
the clock of the seasons goes round and around.
Round and around, round and around;
the clock of the seasons goes round and around.

The Nature of Reality
(Written 21st July, 2014)

Vivienne and Eric (Viv and El) were the perfect couple. They had been together for ages. El was a good looker, a bit of an athlete, and Viv was no slouch either. They had a beautiful home, snug in a warm fold in the land, and they had many friends and relatives.

It was Friday evening, another Friday evening, and Viv was at home tidying up as usual while El had gone off to his favourite watering hole. That night she dined alone. This was becoming a regular occurrence as El seemed to go off for a drink at the same place almost every day just lately. The sun was just about to set in a big red sky when El came home, bounding along with that bouncy joyful stride.

"Hi, Honey, I'm home." he smiled.

"Yes, I can see that." she sighed.

"Oh, don't be like that, sweetheart," he turned on the charm, "I've missed you."

"Eric," she said, "I'm fed up, I don't know why you keep going to the nasty end of town, to that shit-hole, when there's a perfectly good place just around the corner, over that little hill. It's much nicer there, and you know I'll even come with you."

"Viv, darlin' don't moan. I like it down there, and you know that Miriam and Gerald go there, and if it's good enough for toffs like them it's good enough for both of us."

"I might have guessed that you'd mention that tart. Don't you know that madam Miriam has a soft spot for you? She' always sniffing round you. And gormless Gerald's too thick to see the way she smarms all over you."

"But Viv, it's just a bit of harmless flirting. There's no harm in it. You know it's you I love."

Vivienne knew that moaning at her partner wouldn't do any good. She sighed, "OK, Sorry, but please, at least give the other place a moments thought."

"OK sweetheart, just for you."

He lurched towards her with that familiar look on his face. His body language spoke volumes. She could smell his breath.

"Oh, my God, and that's the other thing. You always stink when you come back from that shit-hole."

"Oh, but you know that you still love me just as I am." he smiled that smile.

She knew what was going to happen next, and she knew that she wouldn't be able to stop it.

"I suppose you've eaten?" she asked.

"Yeah! There was this new takeaway just up the road; I'm as full as a pelican's beak."

After he had eaten his fill, there was only one thing on his mind.

"Here we go again." she thought. This is where the nightly ritual began, and it was always the same.

"D'you fancy making some babies then?" he grinned.

It wasn't much of a chat up line, but he didn't have anything better in his repertoire.

Just as many times before she succumbed to his charms and then predictably he fell instantly asleep.

It was Saturday evening, another Saturday evening, and Viv had a very determined look on her face.

"Right Eric," she said, "Tonight were going just around the corner, over that little hill, to my favourite watering hole."

"But, but, I don't want to, sweetheart. Oh, don't make me go there. Miriam and Gerald won't be there. None of my mates go there, and we'll be strangers."

"Eric, I am not taking no for an answer. I've made up my mind Eric. Now come on."

She dragged him in the opposite direction to his desires, and he had no choice. Reluctantly he hopped along as instructed.

Some time later, they returned.

"There that wasn't too bad, was it?" she asked, "And you don't smell as bad as you usually do."

"If you say so," he answered with an air of resignation," But that takeaway on the home trail tasted a bit funny. I don't feel very well, I'm going to bed early tonight."

"You mean you don't want to make babies, then?"

"Don't be stupid woman, that's what I was put on this Earth for." he replied grabbing her, and without any sweet words or foreplay taking her roughly and quickly.

Soon they were both asleep.

And that was it! They never woke up. There was no Sunday morning, not another Sunday morning.

Vivienne and Eric were dead, all their babies were dead, and soon Miriam and Eric would also be dead. None of them knew that the previous evening just before they had gone to their respective watering holes chemical warfare had broken out against their species, and they had been viciously and arbitrarily poisoned.

Reporters notes:

The species can only mate after feeding.

The species has legs designed for jumping great distances and mouthparts designed to suck blood.

The species is required to find a source of moisture once every day by paying a visit to the eyes or the anus of the host.

Ctenocephalides canis is an ectoparasite that lives in a wide variety of animal environments including dogs.

Cardiac Arrest
(A talking blues)
(Written June 1996)

Well, all day long I hadn't felt my best,
Had an elephant sleeping on my chest,
I found it hard to catch my breath,
I didn't know it was a matter of life and death.
I thought about what it might be,
Serious indigestion,
Influenza,
Or even, Mad Cow Disease.

By that evening I felt a bit worse,
Lost my appetite, but had a big thirst,
Had a touch of the Delhi belly,
Spent an active evening watching telly.
Same old crap,
Coronation Street,
Heartbeat,
London's Burning,
Heart of the matter,
I got bored,
So I went to bed.

Well, I woke up in the middle of the night,
Feeling like I'd had a fright,
I said "I don't feel too good at all."
"You'd better take me to hospital."
Broomfield, That is,

Not too far away,
Nevertheless, better get me there,
Pretty damn quick.

I got in the car and we started to drive,
I felt like a man who was barely alive,
Last thing I remember as we rode,
Was bouncing on the cats eyes in the middle of the road.
The wife was grateful,
Most unusual,
I didn't criticise her driving,
Not even once.

Well I walked into A and E,
And only moment later it hit me,
Had VF and MI,
Didn't know if I'd live to die.
Well, I didn't go down no long white tunnel,
And I didn't see any angels,
And I didn't hear Aled Jones singing,
Or Kiri Tekanawa,
I survived the heart attack,
But them abbreviations nearly got me though.

Well, if I'd wanted to die and leave a space,
I'd picked the wrong time, and I'd picked the wrong place,
I went to the door, and I gave a knock,
And then they gave me an electric shock.
Defribulator that is,
Can't recommend it,
Just like a bolt of lightning,
ZAP! POW!

They'd torn my favourite T-shirt off,
So I took a breath, and I gave a cough,
That Frankenstein electric whack,
Had done the trick and brought me back.

Minus my T-shirt,
With two burned nipples,
And a broken shoulder,
Well,
T-shirt,
Shoulder,
Nipples,
Small price to pay,
For being alive!

When I came round in a Coronary Care bed,
I knew I was alive, but I felt like I was dead,
I couldn't recognise anyone,
But at least that elephant had upped and gone.

Been replaced, by snakes and ladders,
Wires for monitors, tubes for drips,
Aspirin, Heparin, Streptokinase,
Oxygen and GTN spray,
And the mask on my face,
In case, anyone recognised me.
In CCU there's TLC,
Lots of drugs and ECG's,
Lots of nurses, there to please,
And an endless stream of lukewarm tea.
Yep, it's the universal cure all,
Had a heart attack?
Have a cup of tea,
You'll feel much better then,
Go on, you know it makes sense.

Pretty soon they were giving me advice,
All about diet and exercise,
All about stress and cholesterol,
Giving up smoking and alcohol,
I told 'em to close the barn door,
That horse is long gone,
Anyway, in my case it's hereditary,
Thanks Dad!

Fully advised and feeling better,
Soon they gave me a discharge letter,
Said don't you come back here no more.
Now pack your bags, there's the door.
I went home; it was a sunny day,
Ate loads of fruit and vegetables,
No steak and chips,
Took long walks,
Didn't smoke or drink,
Slept a lot,
Didn't drive, avoided stress,
Couldn't play golf,
Nearly died of boredom!

Two months later free of stress,
They called me in for a Treadmill Test,
We'll speed it up as you go along,
If you do 12 minutes there's nothing wrong.
I did eleven and a half,
They weren't happy,
Said I'd need an Angiogram,
I told 'em I already had a stereo system.

The days were long and I felt fine,
I played golf from time to time,
Today, tomorrow and the following day,
I felt fine there was golf to play.
Now sometimes when I didn't play,
I just dreamt about it,
And sometimes when I did play,
It was more like a nightmare.

Well, I went to Bart's for the Angiogram,
Enjoyed it all, didn't give a damn,
Till the man came round for the consultation,
Told me I needed a by-pass operation.
I didn't believe him,
So, he said it again,
Told me not to worry though,
There's a 12 month waiting list,
I didn't feel so bad then.

Well, a year passed, and I got older,
Autumn came, and it got colder,
Then one day just by chance,
I was out there playing golf in France,
That old elephant came back again,
This time he kicked me in the chest,
I was upset,
I'd only played four holes.

Well, I laid down on the clubhouse floor,
Adding up my handicap score,
Teams of medics all around,
Try to get me safe and sound.
Well, I didn't pass out, or faint, or vomit,
I felt every needle,
Gasped for every breath,
I wasn't much help,

I was too busy,
Looking for a long white tunnel,
Trying to find a band of angels,
I thought I caught a glimpse of Aled Jones.

Well, I ended up in a hospital bed,
I knew I was alive, but I felt like I was dead,
I couldn't understand anyone,
But at least that elephant had upped and gone.
Been replaced, by snakes and ladders,
Wires for monitors, tubes for drips,
Aspirin, Heparin, RTPA,
Oxygen and GTN spray,
And a mask on my face,
So that's no-one would recognise me,
Looks like deja-vu,
What do you expect, in France?

Ten days later feeling no better,
They gave me a discharge letter,
Said, "Vous ne retournez pas encore".
Now pack "votre baggage, il-y-a la porte."
I went home; it was a cold day,
Had no appetite,
Not even for steak and chips,
Couldn't walk more than a few yards,
Or climb stairs,
Couldn't sleep,
Couldn't drive,
Fully stressed,
Still, I'd waited 12 months now,
It would be my turn soon.

Confident I was top of the list,
Eight days later I saw the cardiologist,
He looked and he sighed, and he too'd and he fro'd,
And he said go home, we'll let you know.
I said thanks for your time Doc,
I feel much better now,
I'll try to get back home before I die,
Don't want to clutter up your surgery,
I know, perhaps I'll have a nice cup of tea!

Well I had six more days at Heartbreak Hotel,
Before they put me in hospital,
When I arrived at my destination,
More than ready to have that operation.
So, I joined the Zipper Club,
And, lived to tell the tale,
Could be a good idea for another song,
Let's say, "Mmmm"
Talking Zipper Club Blues?

The Way I am Now
(Written 7th August, 2018)

The way I am now, just like the way you are now, has been determined over a life, by how much shit you've had to tolerate, and how many times you've been able to smell the flowers. Generally there's a critical imbalance favouring, or should I say flavouring, the shit side of the equation, and the older you get the worse it gets.

Right now the way I am is, fed up, pissed off, annoyed and frustrated.

I am fed up, pissed off, annoyed and frustrated with crap TV. Was it better when we only had 4 channels? Yes!

There are no situation comedies that make you laugh any more, like 'Allo 'Allo, and Only Fools and Horses, Dad's Army, and Fawlty Towers used to make you laugh. There is a lack of quality in the writing. Quality is replaced by persistent use of the f-word. Well, that's just fucking lazy!

Political correctness is succeeding in eliminating the spice, the naughtiness, and the pure essence of comedy. Oh for John Cleese and Connie Booth, Croft and Lloyd, and John Sullivan. Remember, don't mention the Germans?

Aside from comedy, or maybe not, why is Boris Johnson being criticised, pilloried and crucified for saying something that's evidently true? He says that Moslem women who wear the burkha look like letter boxes or bank robbers. Well, do they? Yes, they do!

So, what's wrong with speaking the truth? I thought that one of the reasons why people queue up to come to Britain is because we have freedom of speech. You should be able to say what you like, and if it offends some over sensitive do-gooder minority then why don't they up sticks and go and live somewhere else, like Russia or North Korea?

My answer to all that political correctness is to declare that it's a load of old bollocks. Stick that in your do-gooder pipe and smoke it!

Back to TV now.

It's a truly sad state of affairs to find that there is more quality and substance in TV repeats than anything botched together by the new and modern lot of scribblers. The A - team is being repeated. It's the same plot in every episode, there are 50 thousand bullets flying, usually on a street in Los Angeles, and no-one dies. Murdoch flies in and wreaks havoc, Face charms the women. B. A. Baracus fixes things with sticky tape and drainpipes. The baddies still get their comeuppance, and lo and behold we are entertained. I love it when a plan comes together

What's on the up on TV now then? Reality shows like Big Brother (shite!), I'm a (grossly overpaid) celebrity (looking to regenerate my failing career) get me out of here, (with a big cheque under my arm), and worst of all Love Island. That should be re-titled "Are they going to shag tonight, and will we get good camera shots of the action?" It's scantily clad pornography!

Need I go on?

Yes I will.

I am fed up, pissed off, annoyed and frustrated with the News.

Due to modern communications and the Internet, all the News is here today and gone tomorrow. Nobody cares if 2000 people die in an earthquake, elephants are in danger of becoming extinct, or if climate change is about to kill us all. They are minor items at the tail end of any news bulletin. What's at the front end? Ignoring the obvious one about the weather at the moment; more of that later, it's Brexit. No, it's not! It's Brexit, Brexit, Brexit and more Brexit.

At the root of the Brexit problem that irks us all are 2 things. One is the complete and absolute arrogance of the EU mandarins, especially prime twat, Barnier. Two is the complete and absolute incompetence of all our politicians who are unable, to coin and old phrase, unable to run a piss-up in a brewery.

If ever there was a time when we didn't need politicians but desperately needed statesmen, it is now.

Maybe we should get Noel Edmunds to negotiate with the EU for Britain; he was good at Deal, or no deal. The remoaners want another referendum, and just like the poisoned dwarf, Nicola Sturgeon, they are convinced that the result next time would be to stay in. The leavers are continuously fed with horror stories of "What have you done! We'll be a 3rd World country afterwards, with a lawless society, food shortages, and no say in World affairs. And it will all be your fault!"

Best thing to do is become another Switzerland, neutral, superbly rich, and very clever. After all, the Swiss Bank is still hiding all the Nazi gold and nobody seems to care. The Swiss don't have to have a huge army, fight in any wars, don't get bombed, and they have no need for expensive nuclear weapons.

We are half way towards that situation ourselves already. Our recent spate of armed forces cuts mean we will soon have a Navy of 3 inflatables and a rowing boat, an Army using pea-shooters and catapults, and an Air force that has 3 hang-gliders and a dilapidated Montgolfier hot air balloon. But we will still have a nuclear submarine. Trouble is that no-one will know where it is, because we won't have heard from it for over 5 years.

Need I go on?

Yes I will.

I am fed up, pissed off, annoyed and frustrated that there is no longer any effective scheme of crime and punishment. Due to the do-gooders there are no deterrents to crime. The do-gooders want to analyse why the criminal behaved the way he/she did, with a view to rehabilitation. The criminal is the unfortunate victim of his/her own circumstances. He/she committed a heinous crime because his/her mum didn't give him/her cornflakes for breakfast.

Who bloody cares?

So nowadays, you commit a crime, murder, rape, terrorist atrocities, and you get sent to Butlins - 3 square meals a day, no need to work, TV, mobiles, playstations, gated accommodation, a library, free education, and then you go before a parole board who feels sorry for depriving you of your freedom (what?), and sets you free to commit further crimes.

Whatever happened to the punishment must fit the crime ethos? If you're going to imprison anyone, then give them bread and water, and let them suffer in abject squalor and misery for a week or two.

Minor crimes equals short sharp shock.

Then, let's have a 3 strikes and you are out mentality. After the 3rd crime, conscript them into the Army and send them to Afghanistan, where they can become target practice for the Taliban. For major crimes, don't bother with the expense of keeping them banged up, let them live in tents, surrounded by armed guards, working on heavy construction projects. Breaking rocks in the hot sun. If they run away, shoot them, and if they're repeat offenders then let's bring back Albert Pierpoint.

Need I go on?

Yes I will.

I am fed up, pissed off, annoyed and frustrated by the inability of the authorities to deal with cyclists who ride on the pavement, and ignore all traffic signals. They ride unidentifiable machines (no number plates), and don't contribute to road tax, and they don't need insurance. That's crackpot!

Need I go on?

Yes I will.

I am fed up, pissed off, annoyed and frustrated that they've closed the Army and Navy flyover for 3 weeks to deal with construction issues, and almost everyday there is no-one working on it.

Need I go on?

Yes I will.

I am fed up, pissed off, annoyed and frustrated with the World situation - Trump the chump, Putin the murderer, Kim Jong Un the stupid boy, the Moslem despots of Saudi Arabia, the human rights ignorers of the New China, not to mention the new Fuhrer, Angela Merkel. I don't have a solution to this one. It's too big, too interminable, too complicated.

If we haven't all been seen off by climate change by then, I reckon that by the year of our Emperor 2100 (Note; not year of our Lord, and let's face it nobody knows what the inept religious authorities will make of that), there will be just 4 countries Russia - still run in exactly the same way that the tsars did it, China - the new economic superpower dynasty owning all the World's resources, America - President Clown wondering why and where it all went wrong, and Europe, then known as Greater Germania, and desperately seeking the remains of Adolf Hitler's body to be deified in a Bauhaus megalith building in Berlin and worshipped by all Europeans.

Need I go on?

Yes I will.

What about the weather. I've spent all winter wishing that it would be nice and warm soon, and now I'm moaning that it's too fucking hot and I can't sleep.

Perhaps that's just enough of the ramblings of a grumpy old man.

Maybe, just maybe, I'm not so fed up, pissed off, annoyed and frustrated after all?

I'm alive! I'm breathing in and breathing out, have a place to live, good food to eat, great friends, and I'm enjoying myself.

That's the way I am now.

I've really got nothing to complain about.

I can still smell the flowers.

Lost Child
(Written 8th January, 2006)

In the pale yellow light of a long seaside evening
On a nearly empty beach as a fading sunset dies,
Among the salty tasting tang of dampening sea breezes,
There calls an eerie, lonely sound that pulls my urgent gaze.

Under the lazy swoop and swirl of searching seagull glides,
Blurring at the darkened edge of softly lapping waves,
Along a sandy twilight waterline I faintly spy,
A lost child, solitary, crying by the sea.

Tears are smothered in the swell; cries are muted by the sounds,
She stands up and looks around, there's no one to be seen,
No one to be seen, no one to be seen.

Where are you my child? My Child where are you?
Where are you my child? My Child where are you?

And as the ever moving hand of dark relentless night,
Sweeps away the last few rays of summer's dying light,
A growing mass of deepening shadows swallows up the sound,
And carries her away to be in the warmth of welcome arms.

Tears are smothered in the swell; cries are muted by the sounds,
She was lost, but now she's found, on her way back home,
On her way back home, on her way back home.

Bright day is soon abandoned to cool night's persuading charms,
Her failing soft hold now releases, crying ceases, she is safe,
And all remains in stillness are the gently lapping waves,
In worship to the restless spirits of creation and always.

Tears are smothered in the swell; cries are muted by the sounds,
She was lost, but now she's found, she's on her way back home,
And all remains in stillness are the gently lapping waves,
In worship to the restless spirits of creation and always.

Angel's Holiday
(Written 3rd December, 2012)

It's been a very long, time that I've been training to be an angel, and I have to say that I have enjoyed every minute of it. I remember I started with simple things like sewing crystals made from raindrops on the edges of clouds so that they would all have a silver lining. I spent some time knitting sunbeams together in the right order to make rainbows, and making sure that they were positioned not to touch the ground, so that another angel didn't need to hide a pot of gold at each end. I loved all the nights I spent catching falling stars, and putting them in my pocket, and saving them for a rainy day. I became so good at it Gabriel gave me a special purple pouch to put my falling stars in, so that they would never fade away. They were very special because when I needed them I could use them to perform magical deeds. When I wasn't doing these things I would often be found sitting on a favourite cloud playing on my very own harp, and winding harp strings from angel hair.

Guardian angel duty was always very rewarding. All angels got special assignments looking after someone who needed a bit of help. It was especially wonderful sitting over someone's shoulder, and whispering to them to save them from harm or danger. Sometimes, it was just a matter of creating a timely distraction, like a sudden burst of sunlight through the clouds, or a breath of a cool calming breeze on a very hot day. Maybe a snowflake landing on an eyelash, or a bird suddenly starting to sing in a tree. Anything that was a nice surprise, just to stop them for a moment until the danger had passed. I loved this kind of angel work.

At the end of one day, as I was just idly swinging on a star, I was asked to go and see Gabriel. He told me that he was so pleased with my progress that I had been assigned a holiday.

"What is a holiday?" I asked Gabriel, "And what will I be doing?"

He just said I'd have to wait and see, because holidays were always great mysteries, were randomly allocated, and he couldn't tell me where I would be going, just that it would be very soon. I went back to my duties.

I was carrying some moonbeams home in a jar, wondering what my holiday would be, when I bumped into my old friend Sebastian and he told me what an honour it was if you were assigned a holiday. He advised me that it gave you a chance to do something nasty, wicked or evil, but you had to very, very careful because there were always consequences.

I pressured him into telling me about his last holiday, and after a great deal of persuasion, he swore me to absolute secrecy. Then he said that on his last holiday which had been three aeons and a day ago, he had been sent to Jerusalem, and he had been a Roman soldier on crucifixion duty. The job he was assigned to do was to hammer in one of the nails that put Jesus on the cross. But he wouldn't go into any more detail about what happened. He just said "You'll be fine my friend, if you do the right thing!"

When I tried to sleep that night I was nervous and excited, and I kept waking up with a strange word resounding in my head. It started as a whisper, and then each time I woke up it got louder and louder and louder.

"Oswiecim"
  "Oswiecim"
  "OSwiecim"
  "OSWIECIM!"

The next morning when I woke up, I wasn't on my beautiful cloud with a silver lining, sewn by my own fair hand. I was in a very different place. It was a crude wooden hut, and I was wearing a smart black uniform. It was very cold; snow had fallen overnight but was covered by a layer of grey ash. There was an awful burnt, charred, sickly smell. I was very afraid.

Suddenly there was a lot of commotion and shouting outside, and the clanking, squealing, rushing steam noise of a train arriving, and I heard strange words like "Raus! Raus!" and "Schnell! Schnell!" ringing in my ears. The door of my hut burst open, with a rush of icy chill which cut right through me, and then someone came in to get me. He had a stern, grim face and he ushered me out into the cold, and told me where to stand.

Lots of very sad bedraggled people piled off the train, and were quickly led up to a very important looking man at a desk. He waved any man who looked big and strong to his right. And all the puny, or disabled, or weak old men, together with all the women and children, even women with babies, were herded to his left. Any belongings or suitcases they had brought with them were quickly stacked up and then taken away. Anyone who made any fuss or protest was frogmarched behind a nearby wall, and behind that wall I heard screams and shouts and gunshots. Snow and ash were both still falling, and it was bitterly cold. The wind howled cruelly between the buildings in the darkness of a gruesome early morning. There were no smiles, no affection, and no compassion in this terrible place. The left hand queue were led away and ordered to strip off, and when they asked why, they were told with cynical sneering looks, that they were going to be showered and deloused. Eventually they were led down some steps into a big very bare room with water pipes sticking out of the ceiling. Once everybody had been herded inside two sets of heavy double iron doors were closed and a straight iron bar placed across them.

"You! You're new aren't you?" said Mr Important, looking at me

"Yes sir" I responded scared out of my wits.

"You can do the dirty deed then." he instructed.

He snarled each instruction in short sentences and phrases.

"Climb up that ladder to the top of the roof. Up there you'll find a pair of heavy gloves and a mask. Be careful to put them on. Then take one of the cans from the top of the roof. Twist the top, turn it upside down, and drop it through the hole. Leave the gloves and mask up there. Hold your breath. Climb down as quickly as you can."

I did as I was told terrified, to shouts of "Schnell! Schnell!"

Just as I was going to drop the can, Mr Important shouted "Halt!" and everybody ducked.

There was a very loud rumbling noise coming from the East as a stricken plane coughed and spluttered over, flying very low, with thick black smoke belching out of its engine. Everybody looked up and felt sorry for the poor pilot trapped inside, and then it crashed in a ball of flame, and an awful ground shaking explosion a few fields away.

Moments later Mr Important nodded at me and I carried on as instructed.

"Let's go for breakfast, and come back when it's over" suggested one of the black uniforms, "I don't want to listen to THAT again and again." We all shivered our way into another large wooden hut. There was a small wood burning stove in the corner, some bare wooden tables and stools, and at least it was some respite from the all pervading stench of burning, and the unrelenting bitterness of the wind. There was a calendar on the otherwise bare wall, and I sneaked a look at the date. It was December 24th 1943. The calendar didn't have a picture of a lovely landscape, or seascape, or flowers, or happy smiling faces, just a very stern looking man with a peculiar moustache and pure evil in his eyes. We ate quietly, each man a small piece of sausage, a lump of stale bread, and some ersatz coffee.

"A Messerschmitt me109 wasn't it?" questioned one of the black uniforms," Coming back from the Russian front."

Nobody answered. "Poor bastards!" he continued.

Breakfast was over soon enough. "Now the gruesome work begins." muttered another black uniform, as we all moved back out into the cold. He moved the big iron bar, and opened the first set of double iron doors. There was a strange translucent green light just visible through the small cracks in the second set of iron doors. With a great heavy clang he threw them open, and took a deep breath, before stepping down into what was now an every day, several times a day, sight. But instead of the expected pile of contorted bodies, with tortured screaming faces, and the stench of prussic acid and shit, he found the room was empty.

As he focussed his eyes in utter disbelief, and hesitated on the second step down, the green light seemed to swirl like a ghostly whirlpool. Then a stream of a million blindingly bright twinkling stars, curved in a magnificent continuous lightshow, making their way in a glorious triumphant free ribbon up into the blackness of the heavens.

"What's going on?" roared Mr Important.

"I don't know," answered the black uniform in the doorway, "But the room is empty."

"That's impossible!" hurled a now very angry voice.

"Come and look for yourself." was my reply.

All the other black uniformed men stared into the room, and for a short while stood there baffled. What none of them knew, was that when they were all distracted by the plane's swansong overhead, I had quietly and quickly put the can back on the roof, and retightened the top. Then without anyone noticing I took my purple pouch out of my pocket, and dropped that into the hole in the roof instead.

The black uniforms all gathered around Mr Important, and they started shouting and pointing at me. I stood there shivering in the cold, and then they ran over to me still shouting and dragged me away. They tied my hands behind my back and placed me up against a wall. Weapons were primed as they assembled for a firing squad, but even then for some reason all my fear had left me.

I prayed quietly to myself, closed my eyes, and waited for the bullets to rip into me. But as I felt each one go into my heart I found it didn't hurt. No! Not at all!

Each bullet felt like someone was kissing me very gently, and when the last bullet hit me right between the eyes, then the whole universe swirled round and round for what seemed like ages.

When I opened my eyes I was back on my favourite cloud, and Sebastian was sitting next to me. "How was your holiday?" he asked smiling.

"Er, OK" I replied, obviously looking a bit confused.

"You did the right thing, my friend." he smiled again," Or you wouldn't be back here now"

And with that we carried on catching falling stars and putting them in our pockets, and saving them for a rainy day.

Little Red Riding Hood rewritten for 2015
(Written 15th February, 2015)
(The original fairytale the Brothers Grimm)

Little Red Riding Hood walks through the woods to deliver food to her sickly granny; she had the order from her mother to stay strictly on the path. A mean wolf wants to eat the girl and the food in the basket, and he secretly stalks her behind trees, bushes, and shrubs. He approaches her and she naïvely tells him where she is going. He suggests that the girl pick some flowers and while she does he goes to the granny's house and gets in by pretending to be the girl. He swallows the granny whole and waits for the girl, disguised as the granny. When the girl arrives she notices that her granny looks very strange. Little Red then says, "What a deep voice you have!" ("The better to greet you with"), "Goodness, what big eyes you have!" ("The better to see you with"), "And what big hands you have!" ("The better to hug/grab you with"), and lastly, "What a big mouth you have" ("The better to eat you with!"), at which point the wolf jumps out of bed, and swallows her up too. Then he falls asleep. A lumberjack comes to the rescue and with his axe cuts open the sleeping wolf. Little Red Riding Hood and her grandmother emerge unharmed. They fill the wolf's body with heavy stones and when he awakens and tries to flee the stones cause him to collapse and die.

The 2015 rewrite:

"Britney, get down these stairs. Now! This is the third time I've called you."

"But, Mum, I'm busy playing Pet Rescue Saga."

"Brit-ney! For the last time get down here, or I'm warning you, you'll be sorry."

Britney paused the game on her tablet and reluctantly complied with her irate mother's request. At the bottom of the stairs Sandra was red-faced and in no mood for arguments.

"I don't know why you play those stupid Candy Crush games all the time, Britney. You teenagers are all the same; never want to do anything to help. Anyway, I want you run an errand for me. "

"Oh, do I have to, Mum? I want to talk to my friends on Facebook after I've completed this level."

Sandra put her hands to her hips in exasperation, "Well, you won't be doing that when you get back anyway, my girl. It's about time you knuckled down to your geography homework."

Britney frowned, sighed and sat down on the bottom step; defeated.

"Right!" said Sandra, "Take this leftover pizza to your nan. It's ham and pineapple; her favourite. And while you're there, talk to the old girl. She's lonely and needs a bit of company."

"Why don't you go then?"

"Because I'm sending you, and besides I'm busy with my housework."

"Watching Emmerdale, more like."

"That's enough backchat; just take this pizza and go. Now! Be back in about an hour, Go quickly through the park and keep away from the swings and slides where those awful boys hang around drinking cheap cider and shouting abuse at everybody."

The pizza box changed hands and Britney set off, hangdog, disinterested and muttering underneath her breath, "Parents, Who'd have them? Treat me like a kid. I'm a smart 14, not a clumsy 4."

She left the house, strolled to the end of Giro Road and into the Ian Duncan Smith Memorial park, keeping to the path avoiding the bad boys as requested. She found an empty park bench, sat down and began to play Pet Rescue Saga on her mobile phone. After 15 minutes her credit had run out and she had to finish playing. She continued her walk and soon she was outside grandma's neat little bungalow with rambling roses climbing the porch in Geriatric Avenue. She rang the doorbell which played the American national anthem and waited. There was no reply; so she pressed the bell again and it played "Land of Hope and Glory". Then she went round the back to see if her Nan was at home. Peeping through the window she saw no signs of life.

"One more try and then I give up." she told herself, and returned to the front door and pressed the bell again. This time it played "Auld Lang Syne".

Still no reply.

She turned on her heel and went to go home.

As she closed the garden gate a peculiarly dressed old man came out of the bungalow next door.

He had a massive quiff of dyed dark hair and wore a sparkly onesy unzipped to the waist showing his hairy chest. He was wearing what looked liked biker's boots covered in pink glitter.

"Can I help?" he asked.

"I'm looking for me granny," Britney replied.

"It's Tuesday, She goes to bingo on Tuesdays. Last week she won the £500 jackpot, came home very pleased with herself."

"I've got to deliver this leftover pizza, and Mum will be annoyed if I take it back home."

"What flavour is it?"

"Does that matter? It's ham and pineapple if you must know."

"Wow! That's my favourite. Why don't we just eat it? Tell you what! Come in, and I'll make you a cup of tea, and we'll scoff it together."

Mister Gilter's old eyes brightened and as he smiled at Britney she thought to herself, "Why not?"

"Come on then, call me Barry," he said opening the door, "And what's your name?"

"I'm Britney." she replied as the door was shut behind her.

"That's it, girlie. Sit down and I'll put the kettle on. Do you want milk and sugar in your tea?"

"Yes please, but not too strong."

The teenager looked around the room, and sat on a massive l-shaped red couch. "Ooh! What a big comfy couch you've got." she said.

"All the better to lay down and relax." he replied.

The tea was made and the pizza box was opened. Barry went towards a kitchen draw and came back with a huge sharp knife.

"Ooh! What a massive knife you've got." she said.

"All the better to slice up that delicious looking pizza." he responded.

They began to munch away, and then Britney noticed the music system.

"Ooh! What massive speakers you've got." she said.

"All the better to listen to some good music." he answered. Then he got up and put a CD on.

"Good songs these," he said, "Listen! I think you might like them."

"I'm the leader of the gang, I am" Barry said while looking at Britney, and then he sang with the song, "Do you wanna be in my gang, my gang my gang?"

Britney just smiled, but suddenly she felt a bit uncomfortable at the way the old man was looking at her. She sipped the tea and nibbled at the cold pizza. After a few minutes the next song started.

"Haven't I seen you somewhere before?" he sang along with the CD, staring at the teenager.

"I don't think so." she replied, as he sat next to her on the couch a little too close for comfort. The music was OK, but she didn't like the way he put his arm over the back of the couch behind her.

"I love you love, you love me too love, I love you love me love" blared out of the speakers and he mouthed the words in her direction. Then there was a track with the chorus, "I didn't know I loved you 'til I saw you rock 'n roll", and Barry asked Britney if she wanted to dance.

"No! But I'll have another cup of tea." she replied as a way of getting him to move away from her.

He went to the kitchen and poured two more cuppas for them. When he returned another song started and he sang along grinning at her, "Hello, Hello, I'm back again!"

He jigged about a bit and then plonked himself down again next to her almost knocking the cup out of her hands. His arm went round the back of her again and then he squeezed her shoulder and turned her head towards him with his other hand. Now he was leering at her, fixing his eyes on hers. She started to feel very uneasy and wanted to get away from him. He was sweating; his hands were clammy, and he was breathing all over her face. Another track started and he sang along again.

"Do you wanna touch me? Do you wanna touch me? Do you wanna touch me? Where? There!"

He grabbed her thigh and began to stroke it. She felt her eyes fill with tears. She was scared, and wanted to run back to her mum.

"I think I'd better be going now," she said timidly, "My mum will be worried about me."

His arm came around her waist and he strengthened his hold on her until she felt it difficult to breathe and said, "Don't go now; we were just beginning to get to know each other a little better."

She pushed his face away and turned her head and then she noticed the knife he had cut the pizza with was still on the coffee table. She managed to loosen an elbow from his grip and with all her might forced it under his chin. His head flew back. In one quick movement she wrestled herself free, jumped up, grabbed the knife and pointed it at his fat hairy stomach.

"Get your fucking dirty sweaty hands off me! You perverted old git! I'll cut your wedding tackle clean off right where you're sitting." she screamed, and then she threw the cup of tea in his face.

He recoiled, and squirmed downwards into the cushions of the couch, covering his face with one hand and his crotch with the other.

It was over quickly

She took the opportunity to run for her life, and was out of the door in seconds. At breakneck speed she sped across the park past the drunken bad boys and back to her home. She banged on the door frantically; hoping that the old git had not managed to follow her, but also knowing that he couldn't have run that fast. Her mum opened the door, and Britney burst into tears. She couldn't speak.

Sandra was baffled, "What's wrong, sweetheart?" she asked, "Tell me what's happened."

It was then that she saw the blood stained knife in her daughter's hand.

Punk Piece - Another Turn of the Screw
(Written 5th/7th August, 2012)

I pour scorn on this world where I wasn't born,
Floating in a swamp of mediocrity, pretending to be reality,
An ocean of war and hypocrisy, masquerading as peace and democracy.
Politicians come and go, and tell us what to say and do,
They line their pockets with our dough, and disappear into their altruistic blue.
Communism didn't work because of people's greed,
But capitalism only works to fill the greedy need.
Benefits cut, shops and factories shut, you and me get the chop,
Workers laid off, bosses profits up as they cream it off the top,
Bankers caused the slump, and now they take a dump,
Shitting on the rest of us, still racking up their bonuses.
And all the time they eat away at our freedoms,
Like some insidious little squirming worm,
Slowly, slowly turns the screw,
To every season turn, turn, turn.

What can I say, what can I do, to not offend or undermine?
Political correctness rules the day, to tell the truth may be a crime,
It used to be that you could tell a joke, or have a poke, at anyone just for fun,
Now you can't call something what it is, in case you offend someone.
Once there were queers, now they're called gay,
And they no longer get locked away,
They're all coming out, not staying in, and what they get up to is no more a sin.
And I'm a homophobic because of what I say,
Even though I have no irrational fear of the sordid games they play.
It's now racist to call someone black,

And Irish jokes are a xenophobic attack,
It's the thin end of the wedge, the edge of a ledge, a precipice,
We're about to fall into, a cunning, clever, contrived abyss.

So how long will it be before to say it's raining cats and dogs,
Will be deemed offensive by animal lovers?
Too many cooks spoil the broth, an insult to chefs or Heinz soups?
Give a dog a bad name, to get up the noses of all dogs,
Or just dogs with good names like Rex or Rover?

And now the world of the young is hung with pneumatic, neurotic women,
And pathetic, despotic men,
So the con-trick prevails and we all just fail,
On the same old merry-go-round again.
And they're still eating away at our freedoms,
That insidious little worm still squirming,
To every season turn turn, turn,
Slowly, slowly the inscrutable screw is turning.

I'm persuaded to say nothing, to do much more than less,
Just wallow in apathetic, and revel in the mess,
Swim in the cesspit, climb on the shit-heap, swallow all the crap,
And keep it buttoned, lips sealed, eyes closed, ears plugged, comatose.

Confusion
(Written 10th October, 2017)

Sometimes a day begins with confusion. Never mind, it's not unusual for the weather to be wrong. It's supposed to be raining, but it's sunny and bright and we are on our way to London. It's Sunday, and whoopee! There are trains running. A mortgage is negotiated for the tickets to be bought. Surprisingly, that happens without a fuss or a 15 minute queue, and we go towards the lift for platform one.

I'm amused by the sign on a door which says "Accessible Toilet". I don't see any point in having something called an inaccessible toilet, but I suppose at least it would stay nice and clean. More confusion!

The indicator board on the platform says the 09.58 is on time, and will stop at Ingatestone, Shenfield, Stratford and Liverpool Street. The 12 carriage train rolls in. The carriages at the front look as if they are almost empty, but when the train stops in front of us it is already full. We clamber and scramble aboard like we're in a rugby scrum, falling over cases blocking the gangway, and look around for two vacant seats next to each other. We spy a potential gap in the 3rd row of seats, but there's a moron on the aisle seat with earphones plugged in, and he's reading a magazine. His large sports bag occupies the 2 seats adjacent to him. He knows we are there, but ignores us. We, altogether too politely and apologetically, wait for some movement. There is none. In a panic we step back a few rows and find 2 seats on opposite sides of the aisle.

"If this was Germany or Russia, there'd be a riot over his refusal to move." I say quietly to my partner as the train moves off.

She's French, but agrees with, "The British are too polite, never want to draw attention to themselves, or create a conflict."

It's difficult to make sensible conversation in this uncomfortable crowd, especially as there's lot's of background noise and my hearing aid doesn't like that much.

I start to take in the surroundings and the people there.

The smelly bloke next to me shifts uneasily in his seat sweating and frequently belching. Shift, sweat, belch.

Opposite me there is a young German couple in matching Berghaus jackets reading various parts of the Sunday Times spread across their laps. She reads the sports pages and he examines the home and cookery sheets.

They frequently stop reading and quickly look into each other's eyes. Again and again they smile before he blinks, looks away and carries on reading. That's the cue for her to nuzzle and kiss his neck like a vampire preparing to take a blood feast. Read, stop, look, smile, nuzzle, kiss, read, stop, look, smile, nuzzle, kiss.

I look up and notice that the rolling indicator display at the end of the coach says "This train will shortly be arriving at Witham, where it will be terminated."

"That's funny!" I say to my partner.

"I think they've forgotten to change it," she says, "Probably on the way out the train turned around at Witham. It is Sunday, and there's bound to be engineering works on the line somewhere."

I nod, smile, and go back to studying my fellow travellers.

In the next row sits a Japanese lady occupying 2 seats by sitting in the middle of the bench. She is knitting and chewing gum in a steady synchronised rhythm. She wouldn't look out of place dressed in a kimono and acting at the madam at a gathering of Geisha girls.

Needle click, chew, needle click, and chew.

Ingatestone comes and goes, and the train gets more crowded. Two more passengers attempt unsuccessfully to occupy the seats coveted by the 3 seat moron. They give up and stand up.

Further along, there's group of 4 laddish middle agers being entertained by Mr Loudmouth, who cracks obscene jokes and laughs loudly. He knows that everyone in the carriage can hear him, and he loves it.

The rolling indicator display at the end of the coach repeats, "This train will shortly be arriving at Witham, where it will be terminated." The holiday camp comedian rotates through joke, obscenity, laugh, another joke.

Diagonally across the aisle from me are a couple. He wears a grey suit, open neck white shirt and black well-worn moccasin style shoes. He has a fixed frown on a crater face. His lady has almost black, out of a bottle hair, and is smartly dressed in a white blouse and a short grey skirt over black stockings. His right hand rests permanently on the inside of her left thigh, and he strokes her leg continuously, maybe unconsciously, as she absorbs herself in the world on her mobile phone.

Tap, stroke, tap, tap, stroke, tap, stroke, tap, tap, stroke.

My eyes flit with curiosity from one human interaction to another as if they are all actors in a series of revolving scenes in a Shakespearian play. Perhaps it's "A midsummer day's nightmare" or could it be "As you dislike it".

How I wish the train had been terminated at Witham with all these people on it, because it certainly lives up to a common Sunday train syndrome. I thought it was supposed to rattle along swiftly, and instead it glides excruciatingly slowly towards its next destination. The speed seems to be perfectly synchronised with the movement of the rolling indicator display. If this was anytime after dark I'd expect to hear Gladys Knight and the Pips singing, "You know I'm leaving, on a midnight train to Georgia."

Now, we are at Shenfield and nobody gets off, but more pile on. The cases pile up in the gangway, and space is at a premium as air becomes more sparse.

The doors close and the tannoy says, "All passengers must have a valid ticket before they travel, or they may be subject to a penalty charge." More confusion!

I think to myself, "There's a great deal of point in saying that after the doors have closed and the train has moved off." I smile at my partner. She knows what I am thinking.

Green fields and trees eventually give way to ugly urban sprawl, and there is no let up in the on board entertainment.

Next-to-me-man sweats, shifts and farts.

Heinrich and Heidi Timestein read, stop, look, smile, nuzzle, kiss, and then read, stop, look, smile, nuzzle, and kiss.

They swap pages and occasionally she nibbles his ear.

Mr Cheaplaugh does what he does worst, and his mates all laugh like they'd just been in the pub for 3 hours quaffing copious amounts of lager. Joke, obscenity, laugh, another joke.

Geisha girl's madam chews and knits, and knits and chews.

Crater face remains expressionless as his hand creeps further up his girlfriend's leg. Is she on Facebook, or playing Candy Crush Soda?

Tap, stroke, tap, tap, stroke, tap, stroke, tap, tap, stroke.

Mister 3 seats moron continues to ignore the world and everything in it around him. Earphones on fire, magazine still on the same page. Is he asleep or is he an alien from the planet Supermoron?

More passengers, less space, and more cases, but it doesn't matter because let's not forget it's all not real. This train was terminated at Witham some time ago.

Now our carriage and possibly the rest of the train are like the Jaipur to Jalabad express as we trundle at 22 miles per hour across the wild open places of the Stratford Olympic Park. Is there anyone sitting precariously on the roof and when is the cha waller coming round?

After an age and a day we dawdle idly into the downward incline that leads to release from captivity and the possible sanity of Liverpool Street Station. It's like being drawn inexorably into the bowels of the Earth. I remember the announcement on the tannoy at the beginning of the journey about stopping at Ingatestone, Shenfield, Stratford and Liverpool Street, and taking about 30 minutes. I certainly didn't want to be stuck in this small, crowded space with the strange assortment of passengers for any longer than absolutely necessary. It's been well over 40 minutes. All my trials Lord will soon be over.

A conductor oozes through the door at the end of the carriage as we glide in, better late than never. I wonder if Mister 3 seats moron has paid for all the 3 seats he has commandeered throughout the journey?

The conductor wears a fixed smile under a dark blue hat and white teeth set in a black face, but there's something strange and untouchable about his demeanour. His eyes are fixed like black dots on a domino and his head rotates this way and that robotically and with a whirr as he moves through the aisle. With each ticket checked he says "Thank you, Sir (or Madam). Goodbye!" in a low in a menacingly artificial tone of voice

Then, for some reason he passes by Mr 3 seats moron without checking his ticket, and as soon as that happens the earphones are removed and the sports bag is zipped open.

Suddenly the carriage fills with an acrid pink and purple fog which appears to stream out from Mr 3 seats moron's large sports bag. It swirls around menacingly and quickly fills the air.

Then the slow dawdle of the journey we have experienced all the way changes as we rattle across some points and the train begins to accelerate rapidly. Within seconds the engines are screaming like a jet engine as we approach our final destination.

Nobody moves about or reacts in any way. The circus continues as before, but at a vastly increased velocity.

Sweat, shift and fart, sweat, shift, fart.

Read, stop, look, smile, nuzzle, kiss, read, stop, look, smile, nuzzle, kiss.

Needle click, chew, needle click, and chew.

Joke, obscenity, laugh, another joke.

Tap, stroke, tap, tap, stroke. Tap, stroke, tap, tap, stroke.

Now we are at breakneck speed, and there is no stopping.

There is just enough time for me to stand up. The conductor has a red pencil in his hand, and starts to point it at the collection of heads that project out of the pink and purple fog. He begins to sing in his robotic voice.

"I'm forever blowing bubbles, pretty bubbles in the air."

I quickly learn that it isn't because he a West Ham United supporter. When the point of his pencil touches each head it bursts just as if he were popping large bubbles. As each bubble bursts the fog turns from pink and purple to black. Mister 3 seats moron turns and heads towards me, his face contorted into a wicked threatening smile, and his eyes blazing like shafts of lightning send fierce and painful electronic pulses into me.

Then I look at the rolling indicator display through the blackening fog filled with electricity, and all I see are the orange letters declaring, "This train is........"

"This train is........"

"This train is.......terminated."

Gridlock
(Written 29th December, 2017)

Gather around me all my friends and listen to the tale I tell,
of hold ups in our busy streets and potholes big as hell;
of grief and strife and biting nails, frustration without end,
a problem most insoluble, cause the town's gridlocked again.

Oh the town's gridlocked again, and I just don't know when,
I'll reach my destination, 'cause the town's gridlocked again.

I was on my way into town today, waiting in the usual queue
of traffic stacked back over a mile, and I wasn't sure what I could do,
except twiddle my thumbs and scratch my bum, until the bitter end,
'cause I wasn't going anywhere, while the town's was gridlocked again.

Oh the town's gridlocked again, and I just don't know when,
I'll reach my destination, 'cause the town's gridlocked again.

When I finally made it into the town centre, I was feeling pretty sick.
I was supposed to be at the cinema, to enjoy the latest flick
After hours and hours standing still, the film was over. Amen!
Oh praise the Lord Almighty God, 'cause the town's gridlocked again.

Oh the town's gridlocked again, and I just don't know when,
I'll reach my destination, 'cause the town's gridlocked again.

If you look at the way things are heading now, with prices going sky high?
When they're building here, and building there, and building in the sky.
An influx of badly driven four by fours, seems to be a growing trend,
so the car parks are all chockablock, and the town's gridlocked again.

Oh the town's gridlocked again, and I just don't know when,
I'll reach my destination, 'cause the town's gridlocked again.

So the council put up traffic lights, that will drive you to distraction,
Mini- roundabouts and one-way streets, can't get no satisfaction,
They say it keeps the traffic flowing, and if that's what they intend.
Why is it a stone cold certainty that the town's gridlocked again?

Oh the town's gridlocked again, and I just don't know when,
I'll reach my destination, 'cause the town's gridlocked again.

You'll pay a King's ransom to park in town; that is if you ever arrive.
In my fair town it is understood, I'm in for a slow, slow drive?
Take any road in town anytime, and I'd give it one out of ten.
Perhaps it's mission impossible, because the town's gridlocked again.

Oh the town's gridlocked again, and I just don't know when,
I'll reach my destination, 'cause the town's gridlocked again.

I was on my way to a restaurant, for a Frenchie romantic dinner.
Just my lady, a bottle of wine and me, seemed I was on to a winner.
But I got held up by heavy traffic, and arrived at ten past ten,
She thought that I had stood her up, but the town's was gridlocked again.

Oh the town's gridlocked again, and I just don't know when,
I'll reach my destination, 'cause the town's gridlocked again.

Oh dear! There'd been an accident, and how did it come about?
Why, it's mister selfish on his mobile; I wish he'd leave it out.
He's brought the town to a standstill again, because he couldn't wait to text,
and his utter rank stupidity means, that the town's gridlocked again.

Oh the town's gridlocked again, and I just don't know when,
I'll reach my destination, 'cause the town's gridlocked again.

I'd consider a move to Yorkshire, somewhere in the Moors or Dales.
I'll spruce up the house all nice and posh, and put it up for sale.
If I get my happy motoring there, I'll be able to pretend,
that I don't give a monkey's anymore, when the town's gridlocked again.

Oh the town's gridlocked again, and I just don't know when,
I'll reach my destination, 'cause the town's gridlocked again.

So, if you want to spend a lifetime, frustrated in a steaming queue,
staring hard into the great grey yonder, breathing traffic fumes,
then join your towns biggest club, get in your car, and then,
you'll be tearing out your hair because, the town's gridlocked again.

Oh the town's gridlocked again, and I just don't know when,
I'll reach my destination, 'cause the town's gridlocked again.

Wednesday at the Wine Bar
(Written Wednesday 25th to Friday 27th April 2012)

Wednesday lunchtimes had recently fallen into a regular routine for Tina and Millicent. They had discovered that every Wednesday at 1pm, there was a free concert at the Cramphorn Theatre in Chelmsford. Sometimes it was jazz or classical, saxophone, or piano, or guitar, or some other musical genre. The girls usually met at about 12 noon in the Wine Cellar Bar and Bistro near the Cathedral in Duke Street, and enjoyed a quick lunch from the Lite Bites Menu, before walking up Duke Street to the theatre. That particular Wednesday they were both looking forward to Happy Jazz, with Jeffery Wilson, and Peter Marshall, with a theme of "Birds".

Although Millicent had the exclusive use of her own car, when she was going into Chelmsford, she preferred to walk. So, shortly after getting back from taking Bimbo her crackpot labradoodle for his daily walk, she was off again, making her way through the drizzling rain, to the wine bar via Stump Lane and the Bunny Walk.

Her Spanish beauty friend had set off much earlier in the morning, taking a PAMTAX taxi down to the city centre, to stroll round her favourite shops; Debenhams, River Island, and Monsoon. A few days before she had booked to have her hair done at Toni and Guy's. Unfortunately there had been a mix up over the time of her appointment, and they had contacted her on her mobile while she was in Debenhams, and moved her forward an hour. When she left Toni and Guy's at about 11 am it was raining again and she had time to kill, so she decided to buy a brolly in Marks and Spencer's and walk quickly to the wine bar. By the time Millicent arrived she had been there over 40 minutes, and was just starting on a second bottle of a very tasty Rioja Tempranillo.

Millicent was greeted, with Rioja fumes, and a kiss on both cheeks.

"Hola Meelysont, que tal?"

She was always amused at her friend's pronunciation of her name. It sounded like a lot of money in some European currency. The former model was obviously by now a mite unsteady on her feet," I have been here a while, they mixed up my hair time." she exclaimed.

"Bueno! Never mind. I am here now," responded a slightly damp, smiling Millie, "You've started without me then? Your hair looks lovely."

"Do you want to share this delicious Rioja with me, or do you want something different?"

"No. If you don't mind, I'll have a glass of Chardonnay; I can't drink red wine at lunchtime. It goes to my head."

"OK Meelysont, whatever you say. And what shall we have to eat?"

"Shall we try an option from the buffet menu; that gives us lots of nibbles to share?"

"Estupendo! That will be very nice." she agreed, slurring the orders to a slightly amused barman.

The girls sat down together, and went through the girlie small-talk ritual, and by the time the food arrived Tina was halfway through the 2nd bottle of Rioja. They began foraging their way through the buffet, and Miss Iberia was getting louder and louder. She began to talk about recent events.

"It has been terrible Meelysont, such an upheaval moving to Chelmsford, and then with all the work going on while Tim was away it has been very stressful. I love it in Chelmsford, but we only moved here because of the stalker."

"The stalker?" asked Millicent," You had a stalker? That was back in East Bergholt then?"

"Yes, he was an old boyfriend. Simon was very dark and handsome. I went out with him for about 6 months back in Madrid. He was English though, and he tracked me down when I moved here. It was impossible to get rid off him, even after Tim and I were married."

"Did you get the police involved? Surely they could have done something?"

"We reported him to the police, but as we planned to move to Chelmsford within a few months, they weren't interested."

"That's terrible!" sympathised Millicent, "So what happened after you moved? Did he bother you again?"

She hesitated, and then confided," Yes, somehow Simon tracked me down again within days. I don't know if I should tell you this, even Tim doesn't know, but the man who the police arrested in my garden stealing my goldfish when Tim was away, was the stalker."

Shocked, her friend replied "No I don't believe it!"

"It is true Meelysont, I couldn't tell Tim though." she then laughed and tossed her newly coiffured hair in the air, and added, "Simon was a lovely man when he was my boyfriend, very generous, and very good in bed."

Millie was slightly embarrassed, and after a small pause and a sip of Chardonnay tried to change the subject, saying "How are you enjoying the food, the olives are nice today, aren't they?"

"They're lovely Meely." Tina answered, took a swig of Rioja, and continued, "Spike was very good, when Tim was away. He protected me, made me feel safe. When you first look at him he looks awful, but when you get to know him. Well!"

Then she did it again. She laughed and tossed her head in the air again, and then ran her hand through her hair smiling. She continued with a definite twinkle in her eyes. "He is a very sexy man. I don't believe that he's really a homosexual. It seems such a waste."

Again, her lunch companion was just a little uncomfortable with the conversation, but soaked in the Rioja, she was oblivious to the discomfort she was creating. She took a final glug of wine, looked briefly at the empty bottle, and then said, "You know Meely, I've met lots and lots of different men in my life, especially when I was modelling in Spain. I love Tim in a different way to the others, and we have been married 6 wonderful years now. Oh Meely, don't you ever find married life boring and just long for something different. What about that Polish taxi driver Pavel. He is lovely. Eastern European men, they are very laid back, and he is very fit and athletic."

Even if it wasn't a rhetorical question, there was no answer expected. Millicent wasn't about to directly answer the question anyway. She was shocked at her friend's avalanche of revelations about her men and the way she felt. For a moment she just stared into space, then she answered softly, and without prejudice," No Tina, I'm very happy with my Hugh, and besides, I have three growing teenage boys to look after."

"Of course," slurred Miss Rioja 2012," Gracious me, look at the time; we'd better be going to the theatre."

They walked arm in arm up Duke Street, tiny Millie carrying most of the combined load, and took their seats in the theatre, just before Jeffery and Peter began the first number. A delightful collection of bird influenced jazzy numbers followed, interspersed with some terrible jokes about our feathered friends from Jeffery, which the slightly sober lady enjoyed immensely, while her sozzled friend dozed quietly throughout the whole performance. When the concert was over, Millicent managed to escort her companion out to the foyer, where she ordered and administered several black coffees, while they waited for their taxi to arrive.

Sometime later Tina was gently shoe-horned back into the living room of her house, and Millie went home. She reflected on what had been revealed in the Rioja haze, remembering that the Balls had only married 6 years ago, and that it was obvious that both of them would have history. But she was worried. She really didn't want all the information she'd been presented with, and she didn't know what was best to do with it.

The Merryweather
(Written 23rd March, 2015)

Let me tell you a tale of a ship that set sail
On the cruel Atlantic triangular trade,
From the Liverpool quays,
through the Bay of Biscay,
and down to West Africa way.

The good ship Merryweather was chartered,
with goods for sale or to barter.
with traders or chiefs of the tribes,
loaded with copper and cloth and trinkets and beads,
and alcohol to make ease with the bribes.

Down to the Gambia or around Senegal
or on the Gold Coast shores,
trading with guns and ammunition,
the first leg of the triangle was over and done,
so Captain James prepared the ugliest part of the mission.

Slaves were kidnapped, and set in chain gangs,
by scouring the lands,
for men and women and children.
Then frog marched to the shores,
to be loaded aboard,
in the most appalling conditions.

Packed in head to toe,
they were herded below,
in their hundreds with no way to move.
Chained to the decks,
with wooden yokes round their necks,
and little food and water to soothe.

Then the Merryweather broke the tide,
for a thirty day ride,
across the wide Atlantic Ocean,
and in the bowels of the ship,
frightened slaves were all gripped,
by the relentless miserable motion.

In the middle passage of the triangular voyage,
to nothing like a brave New World,
and with the saddest of human treasure,
The men died of dehydration and disease,
while the women were used by the crew,
at Captain James's pleasure.

James wielded the whip with a devilish smile,
for his crew all the while,
that they sailed on the westward sea.
The natives were danced every now again,
and only the bravest or most foolish of men,
ever attempted to break free?

A few slaves succeeded in loosening their bonds,
and then they jumped terrified overboard,
but every one of them drowned,
'cause there was no way to be found,
to swim hundreds of miles to the shore.

The good ship Merryweather
for Charleston port was bound,
on the fair South Carolina's green fields,
where the slaves would be quarantined on Sullivan's Island,
before their fate was sealed.

Traded in the market like cattle to live,
their lives tending rice, tobacco or sugar cane;
while the ship was washed clean, and
reloaded with rum, molasses and hemp.
bound eastward to Liverpool quays again.

Among the slaves, standing over six feet tall,
was a proud Mandinka warrior called Ki, and
He watched and he listened,
laying plans to escape,
when the Merryweather neared land.

One day's sailing from the Charleston shore,
with the New World in sight and the journey almost done,
Ki broke free from his shackles;
released two more brave men,
And crawled up towards the sun.

He opened the hatch, and
ran over to snatch,
a sword from one of the crew,
but he tripped over a rope,
fell headlong and broke,
both of his long legs in two.

He screamed as he fell,
so the crewman just yelled, and
called for the captain to come.
A slave with two broken legs,
was worth next to nothing he thought,
so he hung him from the yardarm.

When the Mandinka warrior was quite dead,
all the natives were led in their ritual dance on the deck,
where each man could see,
their brave slave comrade Ki,
pale, broken there, hung by the neck.

To press home his wrath,
Captain James finished him off,
by cutting Ki down from the mast, then he
laughed as he chopped him to chunks with his sword,
and threw every piece in the sea.

All the slaves were then whipped,
into the bowels of the ship, and
fastened so tight in their jail,
and every man there,
together trapped in despair,
began to holler and wail.

Suddenly the skies grew dark, and
black clouds filled with rain.
A hurricane blew like the wildest beast in the world.
Batten down the hatches,
make fast for safe haven,
Captain James stern orders were hurled.

The ship spun around, and
pitched deep and high, and
rolled from side to side.
For four hours long,
the crew held fast on,
for the most perilous of rides.

"Abandon ship!" the captain cried,
when the Merryweather was doomed
Then the battered hulk turned turtle,
and all the crew were hurled,
overboard into the raging foam.

On that fateful day every man was drowned,
in the treacherous Atlantic seas,
as the Merryweather was wrecked,
but the saddest loss as the ship was tossed,
were the slaves still trapped below deck.

Packed in head to toe,
they were stranded below,
in their hundreds with no way to escape,
Chained to the decks,
With wooden yokes round their necks,
and to drown where they lay was their fate.

The proud gentlefolk of Charleston,
honoured the dead,
that washed up later on the Carolina's strand,
But only the few,
that made up the crew,
were ever buried on America's land.

Hundreds of slaves met their watery graves,
they all went down with the ship,
never to be seen or heard of again.
And the proud gentlefolk of Charleston,
mourned only the crew who were lost that day,
December 18th 1815, in the hurricane rain.

Some fifty years later,
Abraham Lincoln held true,
to steadfast strong beliefs.
In his own words he said,
"The citizens of the United States
were half slave and half free.

And the most foolish of men
would gather and declare,
no longer could it be,
that America's civil war,
had been fought and been won,
to abolish slavery.
While Lincoln announced that
the time had come,
to grant every man
Whether black or white,
"the blessings of liberty".

On the 18th of December, 1865,
the Thirteenth Amendment was declared,
And every slave in the land,
would hold up his hand,
to remember that day if they dared.

Now when the gales blow ashore,
all the way from the Azores, and
they batter the Carolina strand,
there's a white clapboard church,
standing high on the hill,
where the wild ocean meets the land.

When the wind gets so harsh,
the church starts to sway, and
you can hear the dull thud of an old iron bell.
On the 18th December of every year,
it summons men up from the swell.

The mists swirl around,
as a pale moon is rising, and
You can hear men holler and wail.
A ghost ship glides silent,
Into Sullivan's Island;
The Merryweather comes in, in full sail.

Slaves packed head to toe, and
drowned together below,
in their hundreds with no way to be free,
come dancing in chains round the decks,
wooden yokes still round their necks,
as the ghost ship pulls into the quay.

Then the slaves come ashore,
wading in from the sea, and
the column's two hundred or more,
they'll crawl up the beach, and
at last they'll have reached,
safe haven of Carolina's shore.

For fifty years they were trapped,
beneath the waves worthless and unremembered.
Now at last they're free from their hell,
called by the old iron bell,
on every 18th of December.

And at the head of the trail,
leading the hollers and wails
as the ghostly procession rises from the sea,
it's a proud Mandinka warrior,
who goes by the name of Ki.

Swinging Sixties (A Talking Blues)
(Written 21st December, 2011 to 4th January, 2012)

Welcome to the swinging sixties, some of my halcyon days,
though it was oh so long ago, it still seems like yesterday.
In 1961 the Russians sent a man into space;
Yuri Gagarin he was called.
In April just for fun, strapped into Vostok1,
he spun around the world.
Then the Berlin Wall appeared overnight,
with guns and dogs installed,
And the free world stood there helpless,
and watched the Iron Curtain fall.

Meanwhile back in Merrie England:
I listened to Radio Luxembourg on my new transistor radio
made in Hong Kong, and managed to pass the 13 plus.
I read the Lion the Witch and the Wardrobe.
That year Elvis was King, Ah ha ha!
Elisabeth was Queen,
And gay still meant cheerful and brightly coloured.

Welcome to the swinging sixties, some of my halcyon days,
though it was oh so long ago, it still seems like yesterday.

In 1962 the Russians shipped missiles to Cuba,
and the Yanks went to action stations,
as Khrushchev banged his shoe on the desk
defying the United Nations.

We held our breath, as certain death,
spelled the end of civilisation,
but President Kennedy saved the world from nuclear annihilation.

So the world wasn't saved by a Bruce Willis, Arnold
Swarzeneger, John Wayne or Superman type of character.
Khrushchev was a vodka swilling, erratic, WW2 hero,
and Kennedy was allegedly a womaniser,
having an affair with Marilyn Monroe among others.
Perhaps the moral is, its better to be a lover than a fighter?
If you want to save the world that is!

Welcome to the swinging sixties, some of my halcyon days,
though it was oh so long ago, it still seems like yesterday.

In 1963 Valentina Tereshkova became the first woman in space.
The Beatles 'Please, please me' was released.
Christine Keeler and Mandy Rice Davies
brought our government to its knees.
Bob Dylan told us the times are a-changin',
James Bond came from Russia with love,
And in November in Dallas John Kennedy
went to meet the angels above.

Meanwhile I was in high school
wearing a school uniform 3 sizes too big.
Picture this; turn ups of industrial strength
on both the trousers and blazer,
In English Lit: I was reading a boring book
called Mr Polly by H. G. Wells.
This was soon abandoned for The Gun by C S Forrester,
and Allan Quartermain by Rider Haggard.
When not studying English Lit
I read Lady Chatterley's Lover,
As a result I became so depraved
I joined the Woodpecker darts team,

started smoking and drinking,
and completely forgot where I was
when Kennedy was assassinated.

Welcome to the swinging sixties, some of my halcyon days,
though it was oh so long ago, it still seems like yesterday.

In 1964, this was the year all the oldies groaned.
They didn't understand the words
of the Beatles and the Stones.
'The weekend starts here', they said,
on Ready, Steady, Go,
and all the in-crowd tuned in
to Caroline on pirate radio.

Meanwhile, here in still Great Britain
I could moo-oo-oo-oo-oove like Jagger.
James Bond was in Goldfinger,
and Shirley Bassey sang it,
Harold Wilson became Prime Minister.
He was obsessed with the pound in your pocket,
and the price of pipe tobacco.
My headmaster Mr Harry told me
he didn't like my Beatles hairstyle.
I said that was OK 'cause I
didn't like what was left of his hair.
He sent a letter home to my mum about it.
She wrote back saying
she failed to see how the length of my hair
could affect my academic ability.
I gave up smoking,
and soon after passed 10 GCE 'O' levels.
Mum was delighted, but Mr Harry was outraged,
and refused to present me with my certificates.
Welcome to the swinging sixties, some of my halcyon days,
though it was oh so long ago, it still seems like yesterday.

In 1965 on the only 3 TV channels, still monochrome,
comedy and satire were rife.
There was 'Not so much a programme more a way of life',
'That was the week that was', better known as TW3,
And 'Not only, but also', with Peter Cook and cuddly Dudley.

Meanwhile, in a quiet world for Russians
the media discovered Mods and Rockers.
I went into the 6th form, got bored bored bored with it,
and discovered girls.
Janet Robinson was my first girlfriend,
And her dad ran the local chippie.
Ten minutes of snogging with Janet Fishshop
as she was known,
made you smell like last night's haddock and chips.
Oh! I gave up smoking again.
I took up eating fish and chips!

Welcome to the swinging sixties, some of my halcyon days,
though it was oh so long ago, it still seems like yesterday.

In 1966, if you were a dedicated follower of fashion,
You bought your clothes in Carnaby Street.
The Monkees arrived on our TV's
as America's answer to the Beatles,
Mary Quant and Twiggy promoted the mini skirt.
The World Cup was in England,
and was won by players from West Ham.
President Lyndon B Johnson delighted in napalming Vietnam.

Meanwhile, I left School, started work in London,
bought a Lambretta scooter and became a mod.
I had to leave school because
the uniform was 3 sizes too small.
My trousers , now turnupless, (a new word)

were flapping round my knees,
and a blazer had sleeves on my worn out elbows.
I got drunk for the first time
the night after we won the World Cup.
Good Excuse!
Girls discovered me.
Well! It was the era of the Mini skirt,
women's lib and burning bras,
and most important of all
deodorants for men.
Old Spice and Avon Spicy. Mmm!

Welcome to the swinging sixties, some of my halcyon days,
though it was oh so long ago, it still seems like yesterday.

In 1967 it was all Waterloo sunsets in the summer of Love,
Jimi Hendrix and Purple Haze.
Hippies, and flower power, and San Francisco
filled those heady days.
Experiments with colour TV,
and the first heart transplants were underway,
and in a time of psychedelic
did anybody really see Emily play?

Meanwhile, it wasn't all good,
The Torrey Canyon spilled thousands of tons of oil
all over Cornwall's beaches,
and was bombed by the RAF.
I gave up smoking, and met, loved and lost Denise Frost,
my first serious girlfriend.
The Israelis had a 6-day war
and petrol prices rose to about 1/6 a gallon.
I tell you times were really hard!

I have to point out that after 50 years
I still don't know what a halcyon is?
And I'm convinced that if I ever found out,
I probably wouldn't be able to afford one!

That's actually a complete fib.
I looked it up.
The halcyon is a mythical bird, akin to a kingfisher.
So there!
Isn't education a wonderful thing?
And Wikipaedia!

Welcome to the swinging sixties, some of my halcyon days,
though it was oh so long ago, it still seems like yesterday.

In 1968, it was the year of protest marches
and we shall overcome,
Of CND, and Ban the Bomb, and anti Vietnam.
Martin Luther King was inspired to have a dream,
and was then assassinated,
Dubcek gave the Czechoslovaks hope,
and so the Russians invaded.

Meanwhile, I bought my first guitar,
and learned a few Bob Dylan songs,
I spent most Sundays marching
from Trafalgar Square to Grosvenor Square.
I watched Dads Army and Doctor Who on the telly,
still not colour.
I drank loads of Watneys Red Barrel,
Apollo8 orbited the moon,
and I overcame the urge to give up smoking.

Yeah, I'll tell you more about this halcyon business.
When I wrote this song
I thought about saying 'salad days' instead.
But then, who wants to listen to songs
about lettuce, cucumber and tomatoes?

That's not true either.
Salad days is from Shakespeare's Antony and Cleopatra.
I quote "Salad days" is an idiomatic expression,
referring to a youthful time,
accompanied by the inexperience,
enthusiasm, idealism, innocence,
or indiscretion that one associates with a young person.
That sounds a bit like me!

Welcome to the swinging sixties, some of my kingfisher days,
though it was oh so long ago, it still seems like yesterday.

In 1969 we watched Apollo11 land upon the moon.
Neil Armstrong's giant leap was the first.
Let's not forget, it also made Michael Collins
the loneliest man in the Universe.
Bob Dylan came and played at Isle of Wight,
Concorde took off for its maiden flight,
and John Cleese did those silly walks
on Monty Pythons Flying Circus.

Meanwhile as the sixties drew to a close,
most public telephone boxes were vandalised,
the pubs still closed at half past ten,
and the 3 channels on TV
started about 4 and finished about 11,
and the only fast food restaurant was the Wimpy Bar.
All those pink bits on maps of the world
began to disappear,
as all those ex-colonial countries

renamed themselves, usually with something
starting with the letter Z,
and immediately started their civil war.

On the good side we were told
Engerland swings like a pendulum do?
Ay? What?
You could lay in a bed warmed by your electric blanket,
which you bought with your green shield stamps.
You could stare at the TV test card,
or a fascinating lava lamp.
Then you could wake up to a fresh cuppa
courtesy of your Goblin Teasmade,
which you bought with your Embassy cigarette coupons.
Such wealth, such decadence!

Oh! By the way, did I tell you, I gave up smoking?

Goodbye to the swinging sixties, some of my salad days,
though it was oh so long ago, it still seems like yesterday.

Upside Down
(Written 4th January, 2013)

Imagine that you are at a major conference centre in London. It is 11:30 am, on 22nd December, 2012, and the auditorium is filled with men in well-cut suits, and power-dressed women. All of the assembled throng are bankers, stockbrokers, and financial sector bigwigs high on their generous bonuses, and looking forward to another free junket.

They are waiting to be addressed by the chairman of a government sponsored quango.

A smartly dressed professorial type enters the stage, and the audience lulls quickly to silence. He begins to address his audience.

Allow me to introduce myself, and the reason why I am here having the privilege of talking to you today.

First of all my name is Professor Mac Sasiti, and my credentials are well known as a regular contributor to an extensive range of governmental research projects, not only in Britain, but also throughout the European Economic Community.

I am so glad to have the opportunity to report to you today the universally important findings of our latest research project.

So, let me begin by telling you how this project came about, and then as I explain further, I am sure you will realise why it is so important to our future, our children's future, and our children's children's future. To put no finer point upon it, what I shall shortly illustrate to you today, will fundamentally affect the continued development and survival of the human race.

Six months ago, I met with Deputy Prime Minister, Nick Clegg at 10, Downing Street as he was worried about the predictions of the Mayan civilisation that the world would come to an end on 21st December, 2012.

Various hypothesis were put forward as to how the end would manifest itself, and these included, an interaction between Earth and the black hole at the centre of our galaxy, and the collision of the Earth with a planet called Nibiru. But Mr Clegg was particularly concerned that the United States government believed that when the Earth crossed the middle of the solar system on that potentially fateful date, that there would be a shift in magnetic poles from the ends of the earth, causing a reversal in accepted scientific principles. We would all no doubt agree that such an outcome would be most worrying.

To this end, and after much discussion over large quantities of the fine Newcastle Exhibition strong ale, available in the House of Commons bar, we agreed to hastily form two essential committees, generously aided by a government grant of £10.5 million.

These committees would be the Conference for Research into Accepted Principles (to been known as CRAP) charged with the responsibility to investigate and experiment, and the Service for the Handling and Interpretation of Terminological Expressions (to been known as SHITE) being the reporting arm of the project. Time was of the essence, and so to expedite the project we enlisted the help of the very eminent Norwegian Scientist Doctor Yllis Rekcuf and his trusty assistant Laer Dnebonk who have many years experience of research in this field.

Now, ladies and gentlemen our research portfolio was indeed extensive, and so in the interests of brevity, I propose to deal exclusively here with the main points.

Today I, as the chairman of SHITE, am proud to report, a few of the findings of our CRAP research team.

We at CRAP quickly began to refine our parameters, and to then focus our attention on an investigation into the principles of Upside Down, Back to Front, and Inside Out.

Our first discussion at CRAP centred around the assertion, offered by some members of the committee, that if the world were turned upside down, we in Britain would all be Australian. That our weather would be infinitely better, as would perhaps our beer, but on the down side we would find ourselves eating kangaroo burgers and crocodile sausages. We would be much more successful at cricket, tennis, and other summer sports, but totally inept at International Football. After much debate, it was concluded that as far as football was concerned, the British public would not notice a significant difference.

Secondly, we at CRAP investigated the possibility of gravity turning upside down. It was suggested that this would solve our economic crisis overnight, because all the money would fall out of the rich people's pockets, and if we could develop a mechanism for collecting this money the Exchequer would indeed find itself in an enviable and advantageous position. However, it was pointed out that the money would also fall out of all the poor people's pockets, and therefore this principle would not prove popular with the less wealthy, and in particular the working classes. One interesting effect of the reversal of gravity, which was enthusiastically welcomed by all members of the CRAP committee, was the expectation that at least it would stop raining.

In our 3rd CRAP experiment we set out to prove, that in many circumstances the principle of Upside Down, was effectively the same as Back to Front. This proved fairly easy to determine, and if you will bear with me, I shall with your assistance demonstrate our findings now. Note that my assistant Doctor Rekcuf is at this moment putting my overcoat on me back to front. But having done that, if I lie down flat on the floor you will note that my overcoat will indeed be upside down. By applying the simple principle of movement, from a perpendicular to a horizontal position, I can say that the theory is proven beyond any doubt.

Now, while Doctor Rekcuf removes my overcoat, let me tell you that this experiment was conducted not only with coats of many types, but also items of clothing worn by men, women and children, and in a few cases by monkeys, chimpanzees, and gorillas. It was found to be proven, when also using shirts, trousers, and cardigans. Interestingly we also discovered at CRAP that if one puts one's underpants on inside out, that they were in principle already upside down, and this was also the case with tights and socks. The back to front/upside down theory was also proven with knickers, and stockings, and I personally can confirm this finding to be absolutely true.

We conducted an enormous range of other experiments, which I regret I do not have the time to outline to you today. So again, ladies and gentlemen in the interests of brevity, and in the certain knowledge that we are all short of time, I shall summarise and conclude with some of our other most significant findings:-

1) We discovered that if all the chips fried on a Friday night in Newcastle were piled up from the Earth to reach the Moon, end to end and upside down, the people of Newcastle would still manage to eat them all.

2) We concluded that if all the actors in the popular television programme The Only Way is Essex with an I Q over 50 were laid end-to-end, either upside down or back to front, on the M25 that there would still be nobody to run over.

3) We tackled the intriguing problem of why, when one drops a piece of toast, it always lands butter side down. We were able to refine through extensive experimentation that toast would never land on its edge and stay there, whether it was laid back to front or upside down. Therefore we resolved that the best way to tackle this problem would be; to either not butter the toast at all, or to butter both sides.

and possibly most interesting of all:

4) We have determined that the growing incidence of homosexuality throughout the world can be explained by an apparent confusion between Front Bottom and BackSide.

I am eternally grateful to the British Government, and to Nick Clegg in particular, for the generous funding of the CRAP and SHITE project, and their continuing support for crucially important undertakings such as this.

I'm afraid there will be no time for questions, as I have to swiftly make my way to Southampton where my new ocean going yacht is ready to weigh anchor, and to set sail for my new home in Italy. But as I retire to my brand new 20 roomed villa in the foothills of the Tuscany mountain range, I thank you for attending and for listening to our findings.

May I leave you with a very profound thought? It is clear that the principles of Upside Down, Back to Front, and Inside Out deserve more research. We at CRAP and SHITE have only begun to scratch the surface.

This paper was always, and will remain, etulosba esnesnon. If you remain unconvinced, and cannot believe me, then please apply the principle of Back to Front to the names of myself and my eminent colleagues.

The smartly dressed professorial type leaves the stage, to tumultuous applause, and critical acclaim. It is now lunchtime, and the men in well-cut suits and the power-dressed women, will now tuck into yet another fine feast financed by the public purse.

Opportunity too good to miss
(Originally titled "A star in my pocket")
(Written 31st January, 2015)

The maze of busy city streets groaned under the late May sunshine, laying like the oppressive weight of an electric blanket over the City. At the up and down extremities, dizzy high perfect blue skies were complemented by oven ready pavements like hotplates in a burger bar. The plate glass frontages of the tall buildings stood like huge radiators. Car bonnets were near blistering in temperatures hot enough to fry rump steaks. The metropolis was a turmoil of sweat and toil, noise and bravado; angry streets full of people too busy and too hot to focus on anything but themselves. On this uncomfortably hot late May day nobody wanted to walk on the sunny side of the street.

Mike Hartson meandered homewards from his office at Connor, Hartson and Bromberger Futures in the City's financial heartland. His apartment was 2 tube stops away, but today of all days he wanted to avoid the black hole of Calcutta that was the London Underground. He could have hailed a cab, but for the third time in a year one of the utility companies was busy digging up a section of roads around the area where he lived. He didn't care if it was water, gas, electricity or fibre-optics; it was just another bloody inconvenience.

In the late afternoon there had been no let up in the heat, and as he arrived back at his 7th floor luxury apartment he was relieved at having successfully scurried back to his own air-conditioned, protected bolthole. Here it was spacious, open, cool and comfortable. This was his territory, Hartson country; untouched by the parasitic toxins of external influences. It was just the way he wanted it - ultra-modern, all hard, clinically clean surfaces, top of the range furniture and fittings, no frills, no ornaments to gather dust; his world, impregnable and sterile. Every weekday his "daily", the super efficient Audrey Bairstow made sure of that when she cleaned and sterilised the place from top to bottom.

He flicked the Bose sound bar on, selected Mahler's 5th symphony, and quickly discarded his sweat and work stained clothing into Friday's dry cleaning bag, ready for collection by Audrey in the morning. He enjoyed a quick shower with the temperature set just on the edge of cool, washing away the discomfort of the walk home and the mental stresses of the working day. Refreshed, he dressed light and casually in Hollister t-shirt and Armani chinos adorned by his favourite designer labels, and made coffee. Blue Mountain Arabica coffee beans from Jamaica were his elixir of the day, just as Ramey 2008 Chardonnay was his evening ambrosia. Mike didn't comprehend how the world could function without a quality coffee to stimulate the brain cells and a fine wine to titillate and excite the taste buds.

He liked to separate his life into boxes. To him there was company-time and me-time. Now he was on me-time. While at work he focussed totally on his business with no distractions, and as a result he was efficient, successful and sometimes bordering on the edge of ruthless. When he came home he could flick a switch and deal with his personal life completely separately. If anything was going to change that, even temporarily, it would have to be a seismic shift, something world shatteringly important. He attended to his mail, his email, and his mobile messages as Mahler's 3rd movement, Scherzo in D-major, wafted out of the hi-fi system. Then the financial pirate enjoyed the prawn and avocado sourdough club sandwich Audrey had left for him in the fridge.

The i-phone rang and he picked it up with a smile knowing who it would be without looking at the screen.

"Hi, Taylor, how's it going you old untouchable?"

"Great, Mike. Fucking hot, isn't it?"

"Yes it is for the plebs outside, but I'm sitting here in my cool threads with the air-con on full blast, and all the cares of the day washed away. Where are you?"

"Still at work finishing off some last minute jobs. It's been a hell of a day in the financial markets. We've made a few major killings today."

"Christ, mate, you need a better work/life balance. I knocked it on the head over an hour ago, and I bet we made more than you today."

"That may be so, but you don't have a wife that thinks that Harvey Nicholls is her personal boutique, and three fast growing juvenile delinquent sprogs at private schools to accommodate."

"Too busy looking after number one, that's me all over." Mike chuckled.

Taylor Brandon and Mike were old friends; had worked together a few years ago, and sometimes they met on Friday evenings to talk football and women and old times. The Untouchables was the nickname Mike gave to the company that Taylor worked for, because as financial rivals they always seemed to make bigger killings than any other firm in the market. There was always the suspicion of a potentially shady element to some of their dealings. But Mike had always attempted to remain squeaky clean, and avoid controversial transactions. Where there were big bucks to be made he couldn't say that sometimes he hadn't been tempted.

"Anyway, mate," Taylor continued, "I was talking to our senior partner Sir Eric McClintock earlier. You know him, don't you?"

Mike hesitated. Sir Eric was nicknamed Maverick Mack in the trade, and everybody knew two things about him. Number one was that if there was shady deal going down Eric would be somehow involved in it. Number two was that he was head untouchable, the big cheese who never, ever got caught red-handed. A more slippery sod never graced the city dealing platforms, but when it came to filling coffers full of loot there was no equal.

"Yeah!" said Mike, after his pause for thought, "He's old school, but knows how to broker a good deal. What about it?"

"Well, we've got some business we could put your way. It's top secret and only just this side of legal. Could make a magic mountain of gold for both of our outfits. It involves the Iraqis and Saudis in a major oil deal. Interested?"

Mike needed a fleeting second thought, the temptation was too much, and this time, just this once, the lure of a lucrative business arrangement turned him on. "Are you kidding?" he answered, "Course I am."

"Only one problem, mate; we've got to act quickly to set this up and cash in on the deal. It's like; now or never. Can you meet me and Eric at the Captain's Table in Churchill Avenue at 7 sharp?"

"Shit! That's cutting it a bit fine, but if it's going to be big I'd be daft to turn down the opportunity. Tell me, mate, why is it in the Captain's, and not at the office?"

"Er, well, it's like I said, just this side of legal. You know how Eric likes to cover his arse. Going off piste is his way to avoid suspicions."

Mike laughed, "Maverick Mack didn't get where he was by not bending the rules a little here and there."

"It's up to you, mate. Be there on the dot at 7 and we'll be meeting 2 bigwigs from the States lined up to discuss the ins and outs. Be 2 minutes late and you've maybe missed the boat. It's going to be Eric's way or no way. Hate to see you dropping a clanger."

"OK, I'm on my way. But I'm dressed casual; is that alright?"

"Sure thing, mate, good cover, just be there."

Mike grabbed his wallet and keys, put the i-phone in his pocket, and made swiftly for the door. As he moved to the lift shaft his mobile rang again. It was Courtney, his very latest and for him uncharacteristically long term squeeze.

"Shit! She's coming over at 9." he thought. He didn't know if he would be back home by then, but after a few moments deliberation he decided to risk it and not to answer the call.

Courtney left a text message, "Hi Mike, have the wine nicely chilled and me nicely warmed up later. x C"

There were just 25 minutes to get to the meeting, and he didn't reply. He had itchy feet waiting for the lift to arrive, and when at last it swept into view for some annoying reason it went up rather than down. Two minutes later he marched impatiently and with focussed determination across the entrance hall only to be confronted by Charlie Evans shaking his walking stick as if he was waving Mike down. Charlie was the very correct and always polite chairperson of the apartment block's management company.

"Mr Hartson, how are you?"

Charlie's grey wrinkled features displayed a man prematurely aged by city living, pollution, stress and solitary existence.

"OK, Mr Evans."

"Can I remind you that we have a meeting with the freeholders next Thursday to discuss the annual maintenance and cleaning contract?"

"Yes. I got the note you put through the door. I will be there Mr Evans."

"I'm glad to hear that Mr Hartson, but can I just run something past you?"

"I'm sorry, but I'm in a bit of a hurry. Can it wait 'til Thursday?"

The wheels turned excruciatingly slowly as Charlie deliberated, and then he smiled and answered politely," I suppose so; sorry to delay you Mr Hartson."

Mike smiled, gave a cursory wave and stepped out into the sweltering evening air. He moved thankfully onto the shady pavement and attempted to hail a taxi. He glanced at his TAG Heuer Aquaracer watch and thought," That's already 5 minutes wasted."

It was the third attempt at attracting a cabbie's attention that brought the desired result. The passenger climbed in saying "Captain's Table, Churchill Avenue, quickly please!"

"Do me very best guv'nor." said the cabbie.

The black cab weaved this way and that through the maze of streets with their flow disrupted by the road works for the water company. Then progress was abruptly halted by a temporary traffic light which seemed to stay on red for far too long. It took 4 sequences of light changes before the cab moved again with any purpose. Three, four, five, six more changes of direction left and right, and then progress again ground to a full stop.

"There's been an accident up ahead I think," said the driver," I'd turn around, but we're in a one way street. Just have to sit it out. Sorry!"

Mike quickly glanced out of the window and recognised where they were. He jumped out, threw the cabbie a tenner and began to run. Twenty yards away was the entrance to the City oasis of Blenheim Circus Park, and he knew that if he jogged swiftly through from one end to the other he'd be just around the corner from his destination. He glanced at his watch again and muttered, "9 minutes. I can still get there!"

He raced through the black wrought iron gates at the entrance to the park, pounding along the terracotta coloured tarmac, fringed by the early summer flowerbeds, blooming luxuriously with peonies, primula and clematis in neatly arranged bursts of a myriad of colours. The agitated jogger didn't see them or the splendid display of huge blue and pink blooms on the azalea and rhododendron shrubs. He didn't see the happy couples strolling in the shady boughs making for the bandstand. He didn't hear Dave Wilson's Dixieland Warblers improvising their way through another jazz classic. Then he realised he had a lace undone on his Dolce and Gabbana trainers. He flopped quickly down on a park bench to do up the lace, not noticing at first that he had sat next to what looked like pile of dirty clothes. A weather-beaten and grimy face stared at him, showing yellow teeth in a slimy smile.

"Spare us a couple of quid for a cup of tea, guv'nor?" pleaded the vagrant.

Mike got up quickly, and as he resumed his jog he hurled back, "Fuck off, you idle, dirty bastard!"

The semi-circle path through the park continued, passing the beautifully constructed duck pond where the inhabitants were quacking their way through the evening in delighted playful reverie. Soon the ice-cream van was in his sight, and he knew that just after it, around the back of a small parade of lime trees, the path met the other black wrought iron gate that would be his exit to Churchill Avenue and a well earned cold beer in the Captain's Table tavern. The cool shade of the limes was most welcome, as was the relief from the brightness of the light. But what was this?

"Oh No! No! No!" he screamed out loud, "The fucking gate's been locked."

He rattled the bars of his imprisonment in exasperation as if it would do some good, and seriously considered climbing over the top. The barrier to his quest was fringed all around the edge of the park by a metal fence; 7 feet tall and topped with arrow-like spikes. There was no way he could get through or over without the risk of injury. His heart sank as he turned around and jogged back, faster, more furiously. He had 5 minutes to get there, and there was no chance. He would have to make an alternative route through the streets.

Many questions filled his thoughts, "Would it matter if I was a little late? How late would I be if I went back to the entrance and followed the road around the park? Can I make it by 10 past? Would Eric and Taylor wait?"

Henry's Operation
(Written 13th July, 2015)

I'm going to tell you a story of a man called Henry;
he's in his 80's you know.
He joined our gang at the White Horse Writer's Group about a year ago.
We found out he was Jewish, and Sylvia is his wife,
but we don't get tales of barmitzvahs and bagels in his life.
No! Henry sailed the seven seas in his merchant navy days,
but Neptune and Poseidon are not in his watery escapades.
Then he ran a business with second hand cars to be sold,
where all his deals were kosher, and all his wheels were gold.
When Henry tells his stories we find some common themes;
tank commanders in the war,
the courage of the ghurkas,
Vikings rebelling against poetry,
Grand Kings and Berserkers.
And he's in love with Joanna Lumley
and the charitable things she's done,
Even at his advanced years
he'd probably like to give her one.

Poor old Henry's got a problem, and it's not easy to talk about,
so he went to see the quack to sort his problem out.
Doctor Quack went on the attack
and then threw his hands in the air.
He said that there's no way my friend
I'm going to look in there.
I'll send you to see a specialist;

someone who's in the know,
a potholing man from Nottingham
who'll go where I won't go.
You see Henry's predicament was delicate,
and he'd deliberated for some time,
whether he should try to get help from a guy
who goes where the sun don't shine.

The day of destiny arrived
and Henry nearly ran away in fright.
The potholing man from Nottingham donned his overalls
and a helmet with a bright light,
He took a telescope and a camera probe,
a cheese and chutney sandwich and a thermos flask.
He was well prepared for his expedition
'cause he didn't know how long it would last.
After clambering around for quite some time
the expedition returned to base station.
That's when the potholing man from Nottingham
told Henry he'd need an operation.
Then quickly he rushed off,
waving good luck and mazal tov.

On the 6th of July, Henry waved goodbye
to Sylvia and went to meet his doom.
He twiddled his thumbs and thought of Joanna Lumley
as he sat in the waiting room.
Then, later he lay in his hospital bed
just prior to his operation,
as an 8 strong team of doctors and students
gathered round for his pre-op explanation.
The team leader introduced everyone by name,
and they all smiled at Henry polite and inane.

Then they gathered in closer by Henry's bed,
to hear the words of wisdom that were being said.

Now, said the anaesthetic man
with a gas bottle and a face mask in his hand,
"I'm going to put you into a long
and comfortable deep sleep.
It's my job to make sure you don't wake up before
the surgeon's had a good peep
at what's ailing you down below
where Doctor Quack feared to go,
But where the potholing man from Nottingham
told us something that we needed to know."

Well, said the surgeon man
with a selection of scalpels in his hand,
"It's important my dear Henry that you understand,
we are going into the unknown here,
and we don't know what we'll find.
But we're going to do our best
to put your mind and rest,
so I'll lay it on the line.
It's possible that we may have to cut bits of you away
and take them for examination,
But if this comes to pass,
we'll do skin grafts up your arse,
so there'll be no need for too much consternation.

However, I must warn you
that there may be a small problem
you'll experience if we have bad luck.
But I've done this job before
many times with great success
and I'm not a meshuga or a schmuck.
Sadly it's not a curable situation but I seriously doubt
that you will come to any harm.
You see, if we do have to make grafts
we'll be taking the skin
from the lower part of your forearm."

At this point in the consultation the 8 strong team
all sniggered and tried very hard to hide their grins.
Henry was baffled with what they were amused by
and in no mood to be taken in.
He asked, "What's so funny?"
as the team leader checked his watch
indicating it was really time to go.
Then the surgeon looked Henry
straight in his eyes and said,
"I'm sorry to have to tell you,
that it is possible post-op,
that you won't know your arse from your elbow."

Auction (If Things Don't Change)
(Written 17th - 22nd November, 2015)
Essex Chronicle, August 27, 2015

Hotelier Reassures He Has Not Closed Up;
  Concerns as Blue Boar Hotel Is Boarded for 'Refurbishment Work'
  A WELL-KNOWN hotelier has allayed fears that he plans to close Maldon's famous Blue Boar Hotel.
  Concerned residents had noted that the grade two listed building had been boarded up over the past week, sparking worries that it had been set to close down after a recent dispute between owner John Wilsdon and Maldon District Council's planning team.
  Fined at the start of this month, Mr Wilsdon was fined in excess of Pounds 5,000 by Chelmsford Magistrates ' Court over a planning breach at another of his Maldon sites, The Sunny Sailor pub.
  He told the Chronicle the current state of the Boar Blue wasn't linked.
  The 65-year-old from Coach Lane said,
  "Maldon is a town of bloody losers who have nothing better to do than make up stories,"

Tall harvest has been taken in; low stubble has been burned,
stark fields are brown and bare now and autumn leaves have turned.
Vast gathering flocks are heading South in search of gentle sun;
dark heavy skies load up with chills now winter's time has come.
If things don't change they'll stay the same;
will history be to blame?*
Under the hammer we must go; going going gone.**

Somewhere way down in Maldon Town is a place on Silver Street
with a fine Georgian facade.
There's a 14th century oak-beamed inn and a cobbled black courtyard.
In bygone days stage coaches swayed in warm summer and cold winter,
and on the way changed horses here, between Aldgate and Southminster.
If things don't change they'll stay the same;
will history take the blame?
Under the hammer we must go; going going gone.

Six hundred years of history should be safe behind these doors.
Kings and queens may have been seen to walk these hallowed floors.
So can we airbrush history and discard all its legacy,
like a broken tree that's fallen?
Place character and its relics under the hammer,
and sell them off for auction?
If things don't change they'll stay the same;
and who will take the blame?
Under the hammer we must go; going going gone.

Is the Blue Boar to be stripped bare and pillaged;
its ambiance no more,
Its character and charm hung, drawn and quartered
Before it's shown the door?
Will the shiny black cobbles of the courtyard weep,
and be finely glazed with frost,
as if to display the cold heartless way,
that no one counted the cost?
If things don't change they'll stay the same;
Sometimes it's clear where lies the blame!
Under the hammer we must go; going going gone.

Next on Britain's Got Talent
Jesus Christ will be crucified again
for entertainment on Saturday night.
The greatest show on Earth is on

and Simon Cowell's bought the broadcasting rights.
Pretty soon they'll demolish the Pyramids
and sell them off for hardcore,
before they dismantle the Eiffel Tower
to put iron railings along the shore.
If things don't change they'll stay the same;
will history take the blame?
Under the hammer we must go; going going gone.

Is Maldon really a town of bloody losers,
who have nothing better to do than make up stories?
Perhaps the man behind the plan
is determined to destroy the Blue Boar Inn?
There are hidden truths in every move
that sacrifices value on the altar of financial gain;
secrets and lies, pleasure and pain,
laughter and sighs, sunshine and rain.
If things don't change they'll stay the same;
Sometimes it's clear where lies the blame!
Under the hammer we must go; going going gone.

So here we are once again
in winter coats and at the bus stop wait
to wonder how the world will change
as we stand at New Year's gate.
Whatever the future has in store
you can be sure of one thing.
Our world is filled with those who know
the price of everything and the value of nothing.***
So when things don't change they'll stay the same;
in this one case we know who's to blame.
Under the hammer we must go; going going gone.

* *Author unknown*

** *adapted from KNEES UP MOTHER BROWN a traditional party song*
"Knees up Mother Brown, knees up Mother Brown
Under the table you must go, Ee-aye, Ee-aye, Ee-aye-oh
If I catch you bending I'll saw your legs right off
Knees up, knees up never get the breeze up
Knees up Mother Brown"

*** *Oscar Wilde*
'A cynic is a man who knows the price of everything, and the value of nothing.'

A Change from the Norm
(Originally titled "A few days in the life of a man with a Porsche")
(Written Friday 24th to Monday 27th February 2012)

The clock radio alarm burst into life and the familiar voices of Martin and Sue on Heart FM introduced another play of the Black-eyed Peas singing "Tonight's gonna be a good, good night". It was a frosty February 24th, a Friday 8 am, and the usual buzz of activity was starting to well up around the town centre of Chelmsford. In a posh apartment in the Hub, all was as neat and tidy as Norman Noble liked it. Beginning to stir awake, he looked very briefly at the red digits on the face of the alarm. "Hmm 7.59." he muttered. He was never at his best first thing in the morning. Through bleary eyes he noticed there was someone lying next to him in the bed, and propped up on one arm dared to take a peep. His gaze panned slowly from the shapely bosom heaving suggestively with each heavy breath under the expensive duck-down duvet, to a mass of dyed blonde hair and smudged make up. She was still asleep, but only just, and oh that awful garish red lipstick, reminded him of his mum. He rubbed the sleep from his eyes, and focussed a little more bravely. Closer inspection revealed hair greying at the temples, 3 chins, and a slightly wrinkly neck.

"Oh my God!" he recoiled" It's what's-her-name? Errrm, Caroline, from the Two Brewers, Shit! I've been cougared. Oh, how will I live this down?"

Then, she trembled and blinked awake, and looked at him with some surprise. As she moved there was the faint stale whiffy mixture of Malibu and pineapple and cheap Impulse body spray. He smiled a thin nervous smile, and struggled for something to say, thinking in this situation he'd better be polite. He quietly slurred, "Er! Hi sweetie, how was it for you?"

She tried to answer as honestly as she could with a curt, slightly sarcastic, "Wonderful", but what she really thought was, "Only 6 hours too late for it to matter at all."

"Good!" he replied, quickly turning, and sitting up on the side of the bed, and then getting up, ready to go for a quick shower. He had a boyish, inane smile on his face, as he was thinking, "Hung like a horse, that's me."

If he'd said it rather than thought it, she would probably have replied, "Yes you are. Like a sea horse!"

The man in the Hub was a man of taste, especially in women, and he was embarrassed at the way his standards appeared to have suddenly plummeted to the barmaid from the local in his bed. That wasn't him at all. He was attracted to smart, well-dressed girls who could make intelligent conversation and shared the same interests as him. It wasn't that he was looking for Miss Right, at 26 he was enjoying playing the field, and he seldom took any girl on a second date. He knew he was good looking, a fine catch, neatly turned out, and financially magnetic, but he was also nobody's easy touch.

After Susie his first girlfriend, had dumped him for a bloke with Arnold Swarzeneger muscles, and an intellect which would only just rival a goldfish on Valium, he resolved never to fall for anyone ever again. That had happened when he was 17 and still at school. Susie was a year older than him, working at Debenhams in the High Street, and they were together for 4 months. He loved her in the way that only a teenager with a first experience can. So when it was over, he was cut to very small pieces, blown to mangled molecules, devastated beyond any possible redemption. It took him 6 months of heartache and melancholy to dig his way out of the crevasse that he had fallen into. That was when he had decided to never be taken on that painful, excruciating, undermining ride again. Since then, he had never weakened or wavered towards even liking someone. His women were the proverbial notches on the bedpost, temporarily interesting conquests, disposables, and he liked it that way.

After a while he reappeared in the bedroom saying, "I've got to go off to work. Why don't you have a little doze? I'll bring you a coffee before I go, and then you can leave when you're ready. Just let yourself out."

"OK", she replied snuggling back into the bed, thinking "How sweet", not realising in her early morning doziness that all he was doing was making sure they didn't leave his apartment in the Hub together, and have any of his neighbours, or worse still his friends, bump into them,. He cringed at the thought that they might see him and desperate Caroline Bangs in close proximity.

At 8.45 am precisely the Porsche Carrera 911 engine roared, and slid out onto Springfield Road, making for the A12 and Colchester. The driver gunned it on the slip-road at the Cramphorn flyover, looked at his watch, and gave it the turbo large.

"18 minutes, to the office, easy."

He popped out a Coldplay CD, and pushed it into the player.

"Para, para, paradise", sang Chris Martin, and the Porscheman joined in as best he could.

"Barret, barret, barret eyes."

He wasn't in his best singing mode due the busted lip Caroline had inflicted on him just before he left. Perhaps, he shouldn't have stopped and asked "Can you please make sure you leave quietly?"

At least he'd managed to calm her down before he left for work. Well, she seemed calm enough, and he had let her stay in his apartment and get showered and dressed.

The office of NerdiSoft, on the outskirts of Colchester, soon came into view, and he glanced at his watch. It was 9:10 am. He smiled "Right on time, Yeah!"

He leaned over and picked up his leather briefcase, containing all his important papers, and his laptop, and gave himself a congratulatory splash of Erection aftershave. That morning there would be a board meeting. He expected that it would be the usual crew, and that it would follow a standard route.

Company Chairman Tim (Tiny) Balls, the boss, smart, good dark blue suit, silk tie, patent leather shoes, would give his best "We're a big company, in a little office, running on a shoestring, must grow and prosper" speech.

Hugh Ramsbottom the incredibly obese Marketing Director, Norman's uncle, scruffy, old grey suit, no tie, brown shoes, would puff his way through a rain forest of reports justifying the same marketing strategy he'd trumpeted for a least 5 years.

Gordon Bullock (affectionately known as Golden Bollocks) the worst nightmare, the very gay company accountant, dapper, prematurely grey silver hair, 3 piece pin-striped suit, Gucci loafers, would produce graphs, pie-charts and spreadsheets showing the company was still making a healthy profit, and briefly discuss projections for the next financial year.

And then it was him, Norman Noble, the Development Director, tainted with the boardroom in-joke of being addressed by his uncle Hugh as Mr Nobless. But he knew he was the best dressed bloke by far and modern man about town. It was always his bit of the board meeting that mattered most. He was proud of his position, and the way he had acquired it.

Not academically brilliant, but nevertheless shrewd, he had spent all his teenage years, and a few of his twenties, studying the only thing he had ever been good at. He was a self-confessed computer games supernerd. He had dissected every game and sussed out the way to write the software for all of them. He knew every line of code for the programs for Super Mario, Sonic the Hedgehog, Modern Warfare 1, 2 and 3, Grand Theft Auto, Assassins, all of them. He had reached top level on every game he'd ever played, bar none. Nearly four years ago at the age of 23 he had written a game called Viking Ninja Holocaust 9, perfected it, meticulously prepared the artwork etc., and marched up to NerdiSoft chairman Tim Balls at a Computer Exhibition in the Brentwood Centre, and challenged him to beat him at the game. Tiny's computer game skills were legendary, and he had never been beaten, but after 30 minutes of VNH9 (as the creator called it) he was hooked and baffled, and offered the young man a job on the spot.

Now the continued success of the company hung on the young genius' fevered brain, and his next computer game creation, like a spider on a damp autumn morning web. None of the lads had grown fat and lazy on his account. Although the incredibly obese Marketing Director had certainly grown fat and not too lazy. That was however mostly due to his lifestyle.

Norman certainly wouldn't want to become fat and lazy. He had looked after himself. Sure he was top nerd, but he was well-groomed, fairly slim, not unfit, and liked to think of himself as someone waiting for a call (any day now!) from the production team of the next series of The Only Way is Essex. He idolised Mark Bright. He loved every series of Big Brother. And, he hid his Yorkshire upbringing and particularly his Northern accent under a veil of acquired Essexboy speak.

At 9:15 am the TOWIE fan grabbed himself a frappuccino, and sat down next to his chairman's empty seat. Hugh and Gordon didn't acknowledge his arrival, as they were entrenched in an argument about a rumour that was beginning to circulate, that Mo Farah had beaten the Cube and won £250,000 for his foundation. The accountant didn't believe it was possible, but the marketing director was confident that the rumours had been substantiated. They negotiated a £60 bet to be honoured as and when the relevant episode of the Cube was televised. As they argued, the young man's mind wandered while the irritation of another delayed start to a board meeting began to bite, and numb his brain into unconnected thinking. He would much rather have been getting on with something useful, but instead his thoughts swirled around the name NerdiSoft, as he attempted to amuse himself with what it might stand for.

"Nutcases in Essex really daft software? No that might be NerdaSoft. What about, nobody expects radically different software?"

The truth was it was something far more mundane.

"Yes!" he thought, "North Essex Research and Distribution Software! After all, Tiny had only recently moved to Chelmsford from East Bergholt, and when he and Hugh first started the company in Colchester they were mainly a software distribution company with aspirations to start writing their own products."

He came back from his distraction, shuffled in his seat and coughed nervously not to draw too much attention, and hoped that nobody had seen him leave their favourite watering hole, the Two Brewers in Springfield Road, the previous evening with desperate Caroline Bangs. It had been unusual for them to assemble at the Brewers on a Thursday anyway. Fridays were the night they habitually met. He wondered how he'd managed to find himself waking up in the morning with the barmaid beside him. He hadn't been drunk and incapable, so it wasn't a loss of memory problem. Nowadays he only drank Evian water, and isotonic sports drinks. His colleagues ribbed him about it, especially his uncle, who saw bottled water as a huge marketing con, and only drank draft Guinness and real ale. Hugh reminded everybody as often as he could that Evian spelt backwards was "naive", and claimed that only boys drank Lucozade look-alikes. According to him, real men drank real beer; Guinness, bitter, and certainly not what he would describe as "that piss-water called lager."

Norman had only been drunk once in his life. After his very boozy vodka drenched 18th birthday party, he had woken up the next morning stark bollock naked and shackled by hand and foot with chains and padlocks to the top of a bus shelter in Danbury. He couldn't remember a single thing about how he got there till this day, and had vowed never to get in that state again.

The Cube argument began to fizzle out, and Hugh looked up for the first time, and noticed his nephew's busted lip. "Christ, Nobless! What have you done? "Did you trip over your wallet?"

"No!" he insisted, and wanting to cover his tracks." Remember when we left the Brewers last night?"

There was a pause before the answer came.

"Can't remember a thing, far too pissed to care." said Hugh, as Gordon grinned in agreement.

"No change there then." thought a relieved and embarrassed young man.

Then he explained," When I walked back to the Hub some brainless oik was puking in the doorway, so I picked him up and gave him a right pasting. He got a lucky slap on me once, cut my lip, but now he's probably in intensive care, having breakfast through a straw."

They didn't believe him, but both responded with "Nice one Norm!"

Despite his apparent bravado, he began to feel a bit uncomfortable again about having spent the night with Caroline. She wasn't that old, only 34, and she certainly wasn't old enough to be his mother. So why did he feel that he'd been cougared? His mind wandered again to thoughts of how that had happened, and how best to avoid feeling quite this uncomfortable in future.

Just as the chairman came into the room, and silence fell before the meeting began, he settled back on the conclusion that he had let standards slip, and that he should be a bit more selective in future.

The meeting droned on, taking the predictable route through the set pecking order. Although his was always the penultimate report, when it was Norman's turn he was well aware there were only two things keeping the company going. First and foremost were his ideas for new computer games. Secondly, it was the money that his uncle put up for new projects. The supernerd presented early versions of 2 new games he was working on. Everybody loved the ideas he presented for R. McGeddon's Nerd World Apocalypse, and it was gone 11 before they'd all finished playing an embryonic version of Beer Festival Bastards Final Frontier.

The chairman liked to be very matter-of-fact about his business, and had a habit of leaving the most important items till last. As the meeting was about to break up he spoke.

"I'm in the process of tying up a big new deal at the moment, which will put the company on a global footing" he said.

"OK, so we're taking over the world, are we?" joked Hugh, putting his left index finger to his top lip, and raising his right arm in a Hitler salute. The others looked at each other and laughed.

"No, listen boys," interrupted Tiny, also amused by the flippancy, "This is important. In the next few weeks I plan to fly to China for a meeting with Wang Wu Hoo Du Production."

The marketing director couldn't help but chuckle under his hand, which he'd brought down from the Nazi stance, as he carried on listening.

"And then, I'm going straight on to Columbus in the U.S.A. to meet the guys from Softly Softly Catchee Monkey Distribution." he continued.

Hugh never missed an opportunity to illustrate his knowledge of history, so he piped up with a grin, "I'm sorry to have to tell you that Columbus died in 1506, 20th of May I think it was."

The chairman ignored him and said, "I will call another meeting when I've finalised everything, and before I go I'll fill you all in on the details. Needless to say, this is a bit hush, hush at the moment, but it's going to be massive. I don't want the workforce to get wind of this plan yet, because I think we're going to have to leave this little shack, and move to bigger premises."

He took a deep breath and then added, "Oh, and by the way we'll need to re-brand the company. We won't be going global under the NerdiSoft label. I'll explain more about that later."

The chairman left the room with a dramatic wave, and Hugh burst out laughing.

"What a crafty bugger!" he chuckled, "He flies round the world in 8 days at company expense. Who does he think he is, some modern day Phileas Fogg?"

The others knew that was just their fat colleague being himself. The board members also knew that the marketing director was totally aware of what was going on. The meeting broke up, and they all went to attend to their work.

At 4:30 pm Norman left and drove back his favourite route through the country lanes, listening to Coldplay again. He purred the Porsche on its way through Stanway, Tiptree, Maldon, and Hatfield Peveril, before smashing through the gears onto the last bit of the A12. Soon he was back in his pad in the Hub. Desperate Caroline had gone, but not before she'd trashed the bathroom, smudged "ARSEHOLES" in very red lipstick on all the wardrobes, and thrown all 15 pairs of her one night stand's Calvin Klein boxer shorts over the balcony into the River Chelmer. He could see them floating in a line in the reeds, all the way up to Tescos.

"Hmm! Might have to collect them up later, when it's dark?" he thought.

After a quick run out along the Bunny Walk as far as Fifth Avenue and back, he showered, made himself a healthy quorn bolognaise, and was ready to go out to the Two Brewers. He was just about to finish another session of Viking Ninja Holocaust 9 when just as expected the phone rang. It was the familiar voice of his father Stanley.

"Ey Oop son, 'ow yer diddlin'?"

"Alright Dad, how are you?"

"Mustn't grumble, nobody listens anyway."

"Mum alright, is she?"

"Aye son, same as ever."

"What can I do for you Dad?"

"Well, I'm just phonin' oop to remind thee 'bout t' game tomorrow. You know t' 'ockey match yer sister's playin' in. Oh, and yer mum says if yer stayin' for lunch after she'll do yer fav'rit."

"OK Dad, I hadn't forgotten, I'll be there about 10, see you then, love to Mum."

"Bye son, drive carefully."

"Oh, horror of horrors." thought the man in the Hub as he put the phone down, "Not again."

Every couple of weeks his sister, the unfortunately named Cher Noble, played hockey for a local team. She was built like her mother; like Geoff Capes on steroids. In fact she looked a bit like Geoff Capes without the beard. Her hockey team were called the Norfolk Enchants, they always lost, it was always a family affair, and Norman always hated it, but felt obliged to go along. The team's home ground was near Beccles in Suffolk on a paddock near the Gillingham Dam. Cher liked it because it was handy for the Swan Inn, a hotel, pub and restaurant offering South African cuisine. The owners prided themselves on their game steaks of springbok, ostrich, eland and crocodile as well as other South African specialities like Bobotie, Koeksisters and Chakalaka. The hockey girl sometimes indulged in a game steak or two after the match. To say the pitch was out in the open was pure understatement, and sometimes all the families stood there in the freezing cold, trying to drum up some enthusiasm, chanting away. It sounded really encouraging in Stanley's Yorkshire accent "Norfolk Enchants, Norfolk Enchants."

Ms Noble would play her socks off to no avail, come off with badly bruised legs, covered in mud and cowpats in various states of fermentation, and give her brother a big sisterly hug. "Yuk!" It was dire, and it got worse. Whenever he attended a match she always insisted on coming back in his Porsche, to the bungalow near Leiston, on the accurately named New Clear View Estate. She was always covered in excrement, and he would fret about yet another expensive valet for his pride and joy, and wonder how quickly he could get rid of the stink. Mum and Dad Noble usually returned sometime later in their clapped out Mondeo.

Norman loved his parents, but they were the oddest couple on the planet, Stanley, in his heavy tweed suit, thick set, bushy moustache, yellow, fag-stained teeth, unmistakable Yorkshire cliches, and Lisalotte, of German stock, posh frock, too much very red lipstick, pigeon English at best. They had met at the Munich Beer Festival, when he and a group of master butchers, for that was his trade, had gone on his once in a lifetime trip abroad. She was one of those strappingly built serving wenches, a great bustling clod-hopper of a girl, who could carry 8 huge steins of beer without spilling a drop. Having never been abroad before, he mistook her beery bonhomie for some kind of mutual attraction, and had invited her to a bockwurst eating contest. Surprisingly, she had obliged, only to eat him under the table. Sausages were his life's work, and he was gutted when she beat him. But it was the start of a beautiful relationship, and within a month she had moved to Yorkshire, and they had married by special license. Life was kind to both of them, and the butchery business thrived. Then a celebrity chef called Chester Frumental came on the scene. They held him responsible for screwing it up for them, and forcing them to sell up, and retire to Suffolk.

Every year in mid-June Stanley's business had made a fortune after he had perfected what he called the Seasonal Burgundian, a sausage with an unusual, but very popular twang. He guarded a secret recipe, created something with true rarity value, and managed to sell his goods to some very posh shops and restaurants. Even the Queen ordered them from Fortnum & Mason. Only one man in the whole Universe apart from the butcher himself knew the real secret of his success, which had come about through a stroke of good fortune.

Several years back, the authorities had been forced to reroute the storm water drainage system around the village of Ainderby Steeple, where the Nobles lived and ran their business. This had forced the local frog population to find a new migration route to the River Swale not far away from the butcher's premises.

Stanley came home one night quite late from his favourite pub, The Wellington Heifer, which he had affectionately renamed t' Effin Boot, and ran over and squashed thousands of migrating frogs on the road outside. Never one to miss an opportunity for free meat, he wheel-barrowed them all into his shop, and invented a recipe to use them in an exotic foreign sausage. The migration always took place for 10 nights on the trot, and so eventually he had absolutely thousands and thousands of squashed frogs to process. He reasoned that the French ate frogs' legs, and what was the harm in using the whole frog, beautifully tenderised by the tyres of his van, and then made fresh into the finest bangers he could imagine.

The River Swale frog squash was a Stanley Noble windfall.

But after 5 successful years, and local fame and some small fortune, there was an unfortunate slip-up, which quickly developed into a full-blown scandal. The celebrity chef Chester Frumental was appearing on a TV series highlighting regional food throughout Britain, and had come to Yorkshire. He had already acquired notoriety for offering what many considered to be odd choices and combinations of food. He'd suggested that all meat whatever source, as long as it was tasty and non-toxic was up for grabs, including dogs, cats, rodents, birds, reptiles and even goldfish. He appeared on a news programme talking to Stanley and Lisalotte about Yorkshire butchers, and in particular the Seasonal Burgundian sausage.

Lisalotte, never the brightest button in the box, innocently made a reference to "zoze froggy bangers". Pretty soon a grossly exaggerated magnification of the interview got to the front page of the Northallerton Echo, and that was the end. She had a nervous breakdown, and shortly after that the family felt obliged to sell up, and move, and become anonymous. The Nobles only son Norman had to go down South and stay with his uncle Hugh in Chelmsford to finish his schooling. From that day on the family had held the TV chef responsible for their demise. Stanley said at the time "Bloody Frumental 'im of all people, with 'is pretentious crap infested concoctions. Eeee I'm sure 'e was just jealous. 'E wouldn't know a good sausage if one fell on 'is 'ead."

On Saturday at 1 pm, the Porsche screeched to a halt outside the bungalow. The driver was relieved that yet another awful hockey match was over, but annoyed about the state that his sister had put his treasured car in yet again. He persuaded her to get out and have a bath, as the smell of sweat and cowpat was overpowering, and 10 minutes later the oldies arrived in their old Mondeo backfiring onto the drive.

"Come in sohn," said Lisalotte, "Take your shoes off, and pur uz all a drink."

"Zere's some Blue Nun for ous, some Perry wasser for you my dearest boy, and an Adam's beer for you farzer."

"She always gets it wrong." thought Norman, because she never could say Adnam's, but he never corrected her. Far too many Munich October fests having her ears assaulted by very loud oompah bands had taken their toll, and she had developed a slight deafness problem. Nobody referred to this problem, but everybody enjoyed the frequent misunderstandings that occurred as a result. Soon the German feast was ready. The young man hated bockwurst, and he loathed sauerkraut, but scoffed with pretend enthusiasm to please his mum, even though to him the combination tasted like globules of plastic and flakes of disinfectant. Soon after they'd finished the meal mum and sister had quaffed 3 bottles of Blue Nun between them, and were both snoring contentedly, legs akimbo on the sofa. Father and son made for the garden, where usually Stanley would show off his roses and his prize rhubarb, but it was too early in the season, and there wasn't a lot of promise for either roses or rhubarb. In the previous few days the government had declared a drought in the Southeast of England after an almost rainless 6 months. The Yorkshireman loved his garden, and his son appeased him by showing a bit of interest.

"Come and 'ave a butcher's at this" said Stanley, strolling towards his greenhouse and lighting another cigarette. The persistent use of his favourite phrase, "To 'ave a butcher's", was just another cross to bear in the father and son relationship.

"I'm growin' this funny plant for Sid up t' road, you know, 'im what lives in t' flats, 'e sez it's 'erbal; 'elps 'im wi' 'is arthritis".

They entered the greenhouse, damp and humid, and filled floor to ceiling with a prolific green mass of foliage. Norman didn't have the heart to tell his dad what it was. During his teens he had once smoked some wacky baccy, but to him it did the same things as booze, and so it was struck off the list along with alcohol.

The ex-butcher explained further, "Sid dried these leaves and made us some cakes wi' this once, ah tell thee lad, they didn't taste of booze, but I think 'e laced them wi' it. Me and yer mum, both felt like we'd 'ad 10 pints down t' Effin Boot. It took us 5 days t' get back t' feelin' reet again."

The son grinned, and longed for the open road, Coldplay, and a turbo fix. Soon after the greenhouse visit he said his goodbyes and jumped into the car, breathed a big sigh of relief, and burnt some rubber.

"Sixty-two minutes dead on!" he chuckled, pulling into his parking space at the Hub in Chelmsford. A while later, on that Saturday evening he was showered, shaved, preened, moisturised and ready. He had to go commando due to a sudden shortage of boxer shorts. After another generous splash of Erection aftershave he was on his way, down to Brentwood, to Sugar Hut, to try and be spotted by the scouts for The Only Way is Essex.

The next morning the clock radio alarm burst into life, and the familiar voices of somebody other than Martin and Sue of Heart FM introduced another play of "Tonight's gonna be a good, good night". It was Sunday at 8am and the man in the Hub opened one eye and looked very briefly at the red digits on the face of the alarm. "Hmm 7.59." he muttered. Then he realised there was someone lying next to him in the bed, and propped up on one arm dared to take a peep. His gaze panned slowly from the fine bronzed leg sticking out the side of the expensive duvet, to a neat head of dark hair tinted red and the perfect make up. She was still asleep, but only just, and breathed gently through her understated light pink lipstick. He rubbed the sleep from his eyes, and focussed, with a wry smile, a little more keenly. "Blimey! Not bad!" he thought, "Must have been a lucky night."

"Hang on, think quick, what is her name? I've got it, Clarisa. Phew!"

She turned towards him, blinked awake, focussed, and smiled back. As she moved he caught the expensive fragrance of Hugo Boss Deep Red. He maintained a big toothy grin, and quietly whispered "Hi sweetie! How was it for you?"

"It's a bit late to ask now." she thought but answered convincingly, "You were wonderful, big boy."

"Good!" he replied, and quickly turned full towards her, kissed her on the mouth, forgetting all about his busted lip, and enfolded her in his arms.

"Do you fancy a quick replay then?"

"Ooooooohhh! Yeeees!" she enthused.

At about 8:30 am she reappeared, "I've finished in the bathroom now." she grinned, "Sorry, but I've got to nip back home, and then get to Trinity by 9:30. I'm singing in the choir this morning. Will I see you again?"

Norman got up, grinned at her and made his way to the bathroom saying but only half meaning it, "I do hope so."

The luscious feel of the warm water was running all over him from head to foot as she opened the shower door. He leaned forward out of the spray, and she gave him a quick peck on the lips, followed by an affectionate tug on his willy, smiled, turned and went. He didn't quite catch what she said as she left due to the noise of the running water in his ears, but it sounded like "I must go now, (pause) I've got to feed Phyllis".

"Never mind, whatever it was it can wait" he mused, contented. When he thought about it, he was quite pleased with himself. In the space of 2 days, he'd gone from feeling very uncomfortable about bedding Caroline, to feeling very happy waking up next to somebody as classy as Clarisa. Yes! He was back in a familiar saddle.

"More of the same please" he told himself.

On Monday morning 27th February at 10:30 am, the computer games supernerd was back at work. He visited the gents' urinals and was trying to squeeze in alongside his bulky uncle.

"Were you at the Sugar Hut again on Saturday Nobless, we missed you down the Brewers, no one to take the piss out of?"

The young man was puzzled, and replied, "Saturday? Are you going to the Brewers on Saturdays as well? That's three nights on the trot."

"Yeah, I needed a drink, I was pissed off after the City boys had lost 1 - 0 away at bloody Bromley, and dropped to 4th in the table. That's their 19 game run of away wins come to an end as well. They are so frustrating to watch this year. They've been winning away, but can't string a bunch of wins together and do the business at home. If they're not careful they'll be out of the playoffs."

Norman wasn't that interested in football, but humoured his uncle by offering "I don't suppose this cold weather helps; some matches were called off due to frozen pitches; weren't they?"

"Yes. That's right," replied Hugh, "Anyway, answer the question Nobless, where were you?"

"I went to Sugar Hut, picked up this lovely bit of stuff, Clarisa's her name."

The fatman laughed," Good looking bird, dark red tinted hair, nice make up, good perfume, sings in the church choir at Trinity."

"Yeah, that's her, do you know her?" the young man said with a hint of surprise.

"Yes mate, that's Clarisa Hinton, and there's something you should know."

"What's that?"

The fat one stepped back from the urinal, didn't wash his hands, farted enthusiastically, and before he turned and left the room, he raised his hands above his head, and clapped just once, and let out a strange cry like he was a demented seal at a marine park. The fit one looked down, now in panic, and still peeing shrieked, "Oh My God!"

The Man in Dark Glasses
(Written 22nd October, 2015)

The man in dark glasses
was a man of strong principles.
(He spoke in a high voice
because he'd broken his testicles)
He strides around so self-assured,
confident, and invincible.
It's a mystery what lies behind
his determined expression,
but it is clear what we have here
is a man on a mission.

Hush puppies, Ben Sherman shirt,
dirty finger nails, and a goatee beard;
this man he stands out from the crowd
but he doesn't look strange or weird.
He oozes no charismatic charm
but there's something proud and strong
as he steps in quickly through the door
and sweeps softly through the throng.

Could it be that he's a Jihadi terrorist
or an urbane, urban guerrilla,
an unfancy rambling gambling man
or an undercover mercenary killer?

Do we fear him or revere him
or think that he's a threat?
Does he work for Wonga or 118?
Has he come to collect a debt?

He doesn't need a posh Armani suit
and a vest that's bullet proof.
He can answer every difficult question
because he knows the truth.
He's not with the Russian Mafia,
the Cosa Nostra or the mob,
He targets people like you and me,
'cause recruiting is his job.

He gets his instructions from heaven,
a source that's high above;
the only bullets that he fires
are salvation, peace and love.
There's a New Testament in his pocket
and round his neck a cross;
he's hell-bent on a good cause
and the Lord Jesus is his boss.

He'll put an arm over your shoulder
and comfort you in distress;
smile and say "It'll be OK",
and pray to put your mind at rest.
I suppose the bad breath, the moped
and the crucifix were a clue,
'cause he's a hit man for Jesus
and he's looking for you.

Clever Clive and the Mushroom Harvest - The Full Story
(Written by Michael Haley, sometime during 1993/4, and in February 2014)

The story of Clever Clive and the Mushroom Harvest was written for a specific purpose, and for some time was lost amongst forgotten scribbles. Until, in February 2014 I rediscovered it. Having retyped it into the computer, I decided it would be a good idea to write a story around the story to illustrate why I had written it in the first place. At worst it would be an exercise in writing in the first person for a change. So this is a true story written from personal experience.

On 31st December 1992, Woodward the hatchet man with an unfeasibly black wig administered his coup de grace, and made all incumbents of the management structure at the City of Westminster's Information Technology Department redundant. After 2 years of impending doom, it was a welcome relief from a system gradually misappropriated by yes men and incompetents, decaying in quality, and increasingly stagnating into a vast pool of mediocrity.

I was glad it was all over, and after 17 years service received a substantial redundancy and severance payment. The wolf wouldn't be at the door for a long time, but at nearly 44 I soon realised that I was considered too old and far too expensive to get another similar position. My professionally constructed CV was indeed impressive, but whenever the difficult subject of salary arose at all the interviews the frowns and sharp intakes of breath always indicated a thanks but no thanks.

The Job centre caught up with me and I was interviewed by a juvenile snotty faced no-hoper who wouldn't have been capable of recruiting an emperor penguin in Antarctica. He advised me that I didn't qualify for Job Seeker's Allowance, but that I could try for Council Tax Benefit. After filling in the necessary forms and sending them off to Chelmsford Borough Council, I was surprised to find that I qualified for a reduced rate payment.

Six months passed, and I took up a temporary position as a non-professional golfer, and then a letter arrived. To be exact it wasn't a letter, it was a notice from the Council stating that I was in arrears to the tune of over £200 pounds which they intended to collect as a lump sum on the next 1st day of the month.

There was no problem in affording to pay up, but it was a matter of principle.

Several telephone calls over a few days were spent being shuffled between the Revenue and Benefits Sections and getting nowhere.

I kept telling them, "I gave you the information you requested. It was accurate and true. I haven't done anything wrong, and you haven't even had the good grace to apologise for your mistake."

Revenue said, "You are in arrears, and we have a right to collect it all in one go. Don't blame us, it's all Benefits fault."

Benefits said, "Your application wasn't processed properly. It's not our problem if Revenue want to collect the arrears in one go. That's the way the system works.

"Well it's not the way my system works." was my reply.

The next day I went to my Midland bank branch in the High Street, and cancelled the direct debit in favour of the council.

A few days after the next 1st of the month I received a letter from the council, restating my arrears and telling me that their direct debit had been returned unpaid.

In the intervening period I'd wondered how someone in less fortunate financial circumstances than myself might have reacted to the council's unreasonable behaviour. Supposing you were a pensioner scraping around to make ends meet, or someone with severe problems who might become suicidal with worrying about not being able to pay.

If I remember correctly the full name of the Borough Treasurer given on the council letterhead was Clive Whitehead. I decided to write to him personally. In my letter I outlined the facts, without making any appeal to his better nature. My last sentence simply said "Please read the attached story."

And this is the story I attached to my letter:

"Clever Clive and the Mushroom Harvest

Once upon a time in the land on the edge of a large wood there lived a wise old giant called Clive. He was so wise and clever that everybody called him Clever Clive. He had many children, who lived and worked together with him in a lovely big cottage which had been given to him by the Lords of the Giants in the Crown Cyril. The cottage was called the Crown Cyril Ostrich.

His two favourite sons were Rev and Ben. Rev was a tall, strong, dark-haired lad, impetuous and brash, who didn't care about anyone or anything, except the mushroom harvest. Ben was a good-natured fair-skinned gentle boy, who was very keen on fairness and justice.

Whilst Ben would be quiet and understanding in expressing himself, Rev was always outspoken and insensitive. Clever Clive loved his children, and tried hard to keep them all under control.

He, and his family, had been given the job of stock-piling the mushrooms so that the Lords of the Giants who lived in a fantasy land called the Crown Cyril would never run out.

Once a year the Lords of the Giants had a big party where they ate nearly all the mushrooms Clever Clive and his family had gathered. This meant that Clever Clive would have to send out his two sons into the woods to tell the little people who lived under the trees and bushes there, how many mushrooms would need to be picked by each of them to keep the Crown Cyril happy. Clever Clive would work out the sums, Rev would collect and count the mushrooms together, and Ben would make sure that everything was fair, by measuring the legs of the little people. This was so that those with smaller or weaker legs did not have to pick so many mushrooms. Ben and Rev enjoyed their work and the little people did not mind as long as everything was done fairly.

One day when Ben was in a hurry because Clever Clive had promised him an extra mushroom for tea, he took the magic yellow tape measure with him when he went to visit one of the little people called Sadheart, who lived under a fallen tree right in the middle of the wood. Sadheart was told how many mushrooms to pick, and because his legs were so very small he was pleased not to have to pick too many.

So, Sadheart gathered his mushrooms everyday, and sent them to Clever Clive at the Crown Cyril Ostrich.

Some time later, when Rev and Ben checked the mushroom store they found some mushrooms missing. Clever Clive was not pleased with his two sons, and told them to go away and find out where the mushrooms had gone. Rev was feeling lazy and bossy, and he bullied Ben to go out again and measure, with his everyday brown tape measure, all the little people's legs. Ben trudged into the wood and spent all day from dawn till dusk re-measuring. Sure enough, when he came to look under Sadheart's log, he was there fast asleep. So be measured his legs without waking him.

The next day Ben told Rev that there were some mushrooms missing because Sadheart's legs had not been measured properly the first time. Rev stormed into the wood on the back of his fiercest dragon, breathing fire, and found Sadheart still asleep under the log. He roughly shook him awake, and told him to go and get more mushrooms, or he, and Clever Clive, and the Lords of the Giants in the Crown Cyril Ostrich would be very, very, very, angry.

Sadheart shook with fear, and promised to go right away to pick mushrooms and to deliver them to the Crown Cyril Ostrich that evening.

Off he went in search of some mushrooms, but it had been rather cold the previous night, and there were very few to be seen. In his confused and desperate state he picked some toadstools instead.

When he had gathered as much as he could carry, he went back to his humble home and counted them.

"Oh dear ", he said," the Crown Cyril Ostrich will be very angry with me, what shall I do?"

He worried and fretted, and fretted and worried, and couldn't think of a way to keep Rev happy. He knew that if Rev got very angry he made the little people collect all their mushrooms in a huge heavy wheelbarrow, instead of lots of small light paper bags. Sadheart was so tired!

Night time was near, and poor old Sadheart was in deep despair. He ate just one mushroom for his tea and then he fell asleep under a pile of leaves.

Unfortunately, he was so tired and confused, that he ate a toadstool by mistake and later that night he died.

When Rev found out, he demanded more mushrooms from the other little people.

When Ben found out, he was very sorry that he had mixed up his tape measures, but he wouldn't take the blame.

And, when Clever Clive learned that Sadheart had been so worried that he had killed himself, he turned a blind eye, and just made sure that Ben and Rev would tell the same story to the Lords of the Giants in the Crown Cyril.

When the mushroom stock is short because Ben makes a mistake by using the magic yellow tape measure instead of the ordinary brown one, then shouldn't Sadheart should be told first that a mistake has been made, and second that Ben is very sorry. Shouldn't this should happen before Rev demands that all the missing mushrooms be collected.

Perhaps, Clever Clive was not so clever; maybe he didn't get the full story from Rev and Ben.

Did Sadheart have to die needlessly, because Not so Clever Clive always allowed Rev to bully Ben?

Does anybody, including Ben, Rev, Not so Clever Clive, or the Lords of the Giants in the Crown Cyril, know or care which pile of leaves Sadheart is buried under, as long as the mushroom harvest is collected on time."

A few days later I had a phone call.

"Can I speak to Mr Haley, Michael Haley please?"

"You are speaking to him."

"Good morning Mr Haley, my name is Clive Whitehead. I'm the Borough Treasurer. Thank you for your recent letter. Would you mind very much coming in to talk to me about your council tax?"

"No Clive, I think that's probably a good idea."

We arranged a date and a time, and the call was finished politely.

The following week, I put on my best suit and went to the meeting.

"Good morning. I have an appointment with Clive Whitehead."

"Oh yes, follow me Mr Haley." said the receptionist leading me into a large office with a plush carpet on the floor, and quality furniture.

Clive smiled, and we shook hands, and sat down in a circle with two young ladies who represented the Revenue and Benefits Sections. They were introduced to me as mine host poured tea and offered biscuits.

"Would you like to tell us what this is all about Mr Haley." said Clive.

I repeated all my previous arguments including concern for the way the council might provoke a sad reaction from a less privileged customer.

Ms Revenue sneered her text book stance, and looked at me like I was a Tennant's super lager swigger on a park bench.

Ms Benefit smiled sweetly, but wouldn't make any admission of her department's mistake.

Clive listened, and waited for a natural pause. Then he said, "I found your letter very amusing Mr Haley, and I'm well aware that we could make improvements in the way we deal with the public. This is an unfortunate situation, and we can rectify it."

Then he dismissed the two ladies thanking them for their input.

"I think the concerns you've raised in your story are very realistic, and I thank you for bringing them to my attention in an interesting and amusing way." Clive said.

I drank my tea and took another biscuit. He continued.

"In the circumstances I think the best thing would be if you reinstated your direct debit, and we waived your arrears, which as you say are our fault not yours. Would that be OK?"

"Yes, thank you very much." I replied.

Maldon, 11th August, 991
(Written 27th April, 2018)
(1027 years after the battle. Well, better late, than never!)

The lazy, late summer sun began to fall into the sea towards our West, as our long ships eased their quiet, undisturbed course along the middle of the mile wide river. The tide was in favour, pushing the flotilla of warships further into the estuary on the light breeze. A gentle ripple flowed the river's black water slowly towards the destination. Our vessel, Shippy McShipface eased a steady course behind the flagship, "Long Serpent", captained by our leader, and mighty warrior, Olaf Tryggvason.

Another mighty warrior, Valdemar, his long tresses spreading in the breeze, rose to his feet in the leading ship. He thumped his chest, blew a low and penetrating note on his golden horn, and gave a roar from the very bottom of his lungs. There was no mistaking that he demanded attention.

His outstretched right arm pointed to the South, towards an island in the middle of the stream. The flat surrounding land at the river's edges provided no cover for invasion, and the worriers amongst the crew, Gunnar, Steinar, and Ivar, cowered in the bowels of the middle deck.

"Stand up and be seen, you cowardly dogs," shrieked Magnus, "It doesn't matter a maiden's fart if the Anglo-Saxons see us coming up their river. We are under the protection of our Gods. The steadfast and true Norse god of the sea, our faithful Aegir, and Njord our god of the winds and the seas, have brought us all safely here."

Steinar rose slightly, and squirmed his reply.

"To be sure! Oh wise one, we have flown under his glorious flag on many raids along these shores, and into the weak and feeble lands of many enemies, all from our Dane homeland, far and wide, But....."

"But what?"

There was no immediate response as the three worriers stared at each other.

"Why do the three of you cower in fear? We are invincible against such an inept and ill-equipped enemy."

"Have you not heard the stories? They have a warrior in Maldon called Earl Byrhtnoth, and he stands as tall as our long ship masts. He is a fearsome and brutal beast who fights like a cornered brown bear and drinks the blood of his kills while it is still warm. They say that one day in the distant future he will be held up as a great hero, and they will raise a statue to his name on these shores"

Magnus took his staff and began to beat at Gunnar's head. He cowered further down.

The mighty one laughed derisively, "And I suppose he eats babies for breakfast, washed down with flagons of ale brewed from maiden's piss?"

He paused; hands on hips, as if waiting for a response. There was none.

"Don't be so effin' stupid! Who ever heard of any bloke called Bert who fought a battle and won? We'll send Olaf the mighty Pink Poof to take him on single-handed. Now! Get up on your feet and be ready to go ashore, before I slice the three of you into smorgasbord. Our Gods will provide protection. Odin, King of the Norse Gods, God of poetry, battle and death, the all-father, the terrible one, the one-eyed, and the father of battle, will be at our side."

Streams of gold like tassels of liquid silk spread across the ripples of the warm evening waters as fifty Viking sea craft, headed by the flagship "Long Serpent", hauled up to the shallows surrounding the small island.

Lord of the raiders, the Norwegian Olaf Tryggvason, waded ashore first, brandishing his huge axe aloft. He was followed by his standard bearer, Heimdall, his talisman and protector, named after the Watchman of all the Norse gods and owner of the Gjallarhorn. Then the onslaught of men and weapons began to swarm across the flat land, jumping into the water from the armada of long ships, splashing and stumbling ashore yelling a fearsome battle cry, like a tidal wave of pure menace intent on drowning everyone and everything in its path. They rampaged quickly through the island and ensured that it was deserted.

Soon, the sun fell into the waters to the West, the night air cooled, and a thin mist shrouded the Viking landfall. A rough camp was constructed, crude earthwork defences, guarded by hungry men. Viking raiders knew no fear.

Fires were lit to keep warm, and to frighten the Anglo-Saxons, who had assembled on the Southern shores opposite the island's causeway.

"Did you catch a fine haul of fish in the nets on our cruise up this river?" asked Magnus.

"Not bad! But also not sufficient for all of us." replied Snorre, the unruly one.

"These men need food and ale to strengthen their bones before battle. How can we feed them all?

"It's not my problem, Magnus. I am a simple fisherman, and I can only dish out what we've caught today."

"Right!" said Magnus, "Tell Bjorn and Bjorn Again and Ulf to come to my tent immediately."

Snorre went off to look for his comrades. The Bjorns and Ulf were discovered chasing a wild boar.

"Now!" said Magnus, "You three head off into town, and go to the Kebab Shop in the High Street. Tell them you want all the kebabs they can make, and if the shopkeeper makes a fuss about not paying, then tell him you are quite willing to cut him up into little pieces and turn him into kebabs as well."

"Why us?" asked Bjorn.

"Isn't it bleedin'' obvious?" Magnus replied, "Three men with names meaning bear and wolf should be able to find food anywhere they go."

"But what if the Anglo-Saxons capture us?" said Bjorn Again, "After all, the horned helmets are a bit of a giveaway."

"Take them off, and wrap yourselves inside this huge cloak. If anyone stops you then tell them that your name is Edward Bright, the fat man of Maldon."

"Won't they see three heads?"

"Nah! They're too thick to question that. After all they are all effin' inbreds. You won't be the only three headed beasts out there."

"OK mighty one, we'll be as quick as we can. But what about the vicious fire-breathing dragons?"

"Make sure you run very fast."

The Bjorns and Ulf turned to leave. Magnus had a final thought.

"If you can get a dragon to chase you, we'll kill it right here, and eat it. I love a dragon and watercress club sandwich. Mmmm!"

Olaf Tryggvason sat by his fire, warming his hands and reddening his face. His elite warriors were sat in a circle around him, high spirited, laughing, eating their food, and swilling flagons of dark ale.

"Nice little island base this," said Olaf, "I'm going to name it Northey, Isle of the Sea, after our great God, Aegir. Come the morrow we will show Æthelred the Unready, Earl Byrhtnoth, and all his thegns our supremacy. We will conquer their lands; savage their warriors, burn their villages, rape their women, and pillage all their valuables. We will sweep all before us, killing all our enemies. We will give no quarter!"

Battle hardened veterans of Viking raids throughout the Northern shores gave an ear-splitting collective roar of approval, and dispersed to their campsites.

"Can I speak with you, oh wise and mighty one?" whined a puny waif of an excuse for a Viking.

"Oh. What is it now," howled Magnus to Olaf the Pink Poof.

"Two things!"

"What!"

"Well, you know about this rape and pillage business?"

"Yes! What about it?"

"I don't know why you keep picking on me, and putting me on rape. And you know that I'm not that keen. Could I go on pillage for a change?"

Magnus thought for a moment.

"Weak bones like your can't carry anything, and that's why you're on the rape."

"But I don't like doing it. You know that I am not that way inclined."

"Beware Olaf, our comrades all know about your strange habits. It is better that you are inclined at all.

If necessary we can chop off any bits that offend."

A tear came to Olaf the Pink Poof's eyes.

"The second thing?" Magnus asked.

"Don't you see I am losing a lot of weight? I used to be a strong 13 stone, and now I'm a puny and feeble 9 stone."

Magnus laughed.

"I know why that is."

"Why?"

"Number one, you spend all your time running after other men and boys.

Number two; you're the least effective rapist of women ever. You don't rape, you seduce, and all the women of the conquered lands think that if they are going to get bonked, it might as well be by someone who does it nicely. By all the Gods, man, they come to me and ask for you. You are an enigmatic legend of a sex god across our Viking kingdoms."

"Is there more?"

"Yes! Number three, you are a vegan. Whoever heard of a Viking warrior who doesn't eat animal products? You must be the only Viking Vegan on this Earth, and that's the real reason you're so skinny."

"Is that it?"

"Yes! Now go away, and don't bother me again."

When the midnight owl hooted there were over 2,000 Norsemen ashore. Little Northey Island was crowded, noisy and smelly. The casks on all the ale ships had been drained. The little island was devoid of anything that moved or breathed. Everything had been eaten. The fish were all gobbled up. The kebabs had been devoured. The chilli sauce had taken effect. The latrines were filled to overflowing. Even the dragon that had chased Bjorn, Bjorn Again and Ulf back from the High Street had been carved, picked and plucked until its bones were dry. There had been no watercress for Magnus' club sandwich, and he had not retired in the best of spirits. Sleep invaded the assembly. It was a heavy headed, snore filled, fart filled, and groan filled, drunken slumber.

Magnus' eyes were the first to flicker open. He woke Olaf Tryggvason, and sounded the horn to summon his army for battle.

"We'll cross to the mainland Southwards, over the causeway, three abreast, and murder these lily livered Anglo-Saxons in their beds. Get the men assembled, ready for battle, and send out Eirik, Trygve, and Sigurd at the head of the column." Olaf instructed.

A pale, eerie dawn swallowed the slow rise of a reluctant morning sun. Northey Island was obscured in a damp, misty shroud. No birds sang. Water slapped lazily at the shores. Silence preceded the battle. All weapons, axes, spears, swords, bows and arrows, picks, poles, daggers, shovels, and shields were poised and positioned for the onslaught, as Olaf addressed his troops.

"I remind you, my comrades, of the wise words of our illustrious God,

Odin, when he said: Don't leave your weapons lying about behind your back in a field; you never know when you may need, all of sudden, your spear."

He paused, and then goaded at the top of his voice, "When Odin said spear, he meant any weapon, and even a large rock is a weapon in the right hands."

The gathering roared with bravado and aggression.

"What did I tell you last night? Remember? Today we will conquer the Anglo-Saxon lands; savage the warriors, burn the villages, rape the women, and pillage all the valuables. We will sweep all before us, killing all our enemies. We will give no quarter!"

The massed ranks surged forward out onto the narrow causeway to make battle, men clattering their shields in a cacophonous din, and shrieking like demented jackals, as a discordant orchestra of horns blew behind the leaders.

They were met with surprise. The Anglo-Saxons, led by Bryhtnoth and commanded by Æthelred the Unready, were ready. They charged along the causeway, hacking at the Vikings in the front line. Eirik, Trygve, and Sigurd were brutally overwhelmed. and the Valkyries; beautiful women who carried dying warriors to Valhalla, were busy within minutes, as the black river became the red river with the spilled blood of the Norsemen. The furious, bloody battle raged with no let up, and the Anglo-Saxons sensed an easy victory.

"Fall back! Fall Back to the island" shouted Olaf Tryggvason, as the horn blowers sounded a retreat in the full heat of a battle that the Viking warriors couldn't believe they were losing.

Both armies regrouped. The Vikings retreated to the far side of the island, leaving only a token force on the causeway foreshore, while their opposition waited for a signal of surrender.

"It's not the bloody Anglo-Saxons who have beaten us back," whispered Bjorn to Bjorn Again, and Ulf.

"What do you say?" asked Steinar.

"It's those effin kebabs; we've all got the gallops this morning. We can't put up a fight with empty bellies and sore arses."

Olaf Tryggvason gathered his troops around him, and urged, "Men, the Gods are still asleep and have eluded us this early in the day. We have few options. Board our ships and take flight, or fight to the death, or surrender. The honour of our Viking heritage is at stake. If we flee, then our honour will be stained for all time. Men will laugh and say that our mighty army were beaten into submission by a man called Bert, and a King called Ethel.

"No surrender! No surrender! No surrender!" came back from the men.

"Let us wake our Gods, and summon their help. We will call upon Loki, the Sly One, the Trickster, the Shape Changer and the Sky Traveller to help us. We will ask Modgud, the maiden guardian of the bridge over the river Gjoll in Jotenheim to stand on the causeway with us. We will insist that Thor, God of Sky, Thunder God, and Charioteer stand with us and lead us to victory."

"Victory! Victory! Victory!!" came back from the men.

"I have an idea." said Magnus, "The enemy think they have already won. The river runs red with our blood. The bodies of our valiant men have piled up all along the causeway, and it is this causeway that has caused our retreat."

"No retreat! No retreat! No retreat!"

"I will go under a flag of truce, and take Olaf the Pink Poof with me to speak with Bryhtnoth. I will ask him if we can come ashore. He will think we only have a few good men left to resume the battle, and they are weak men like our gay friend. But when we get onto their shore we will turn on them and massacre the whole army."

"Massacre! Massacre! Massacre!"

"We will have Loki on our side. The Trickster will convince Bryhtnoth to fight fairly, and Modgud will be our guardian over the bridge. The Valkyries have carried too many of our dying warriors to Valhalla."

And so it was! The plan was laid, the trick paid off. The final battle raged on the Anglo-Saxon shore, and Bryhtnoth was slain. The ragged remnants of the defeated army fled to the surrounding marshes, and the victors made a quick passage to the highest point in Essex, at Danbury, to bury their dead.

The cowardly vanquished feared a full scale Viking invasion and soon after, King Æthelred decided to buy off the Vikings rather than continue the armed struggle. He made a payment of 10,000 Roman pounds of silver to his victors. This first example of Danegeld in England persuaded the Vikings to go to Switzerland and open a bank account.

The mighty warrior, Valdemar appeared as Voldemort in the Harry Potter books and films.

Olaf Tryggvason led many more raids across the Northern shores, ending up in Iceland, where he bought a pack of twenty burgers and two dozen sausages and invented the barbecue.

Magnus invented the black leather swivel chair, and his ancestors became interrogators to many royal courts including the Spanish Inquisition and the grand court of Torquemada.

Nobody expects the Spanish Inquisition!

Gunnar, Steinar, and Ivar worried their way into early graves, but not before they had become famous as prophets of doom as equally pessimistic as Nostradamus.

Earl Bryhtnoth tried eating babies for breakfast, and became famous throughout Maldon, and indeed had a statue erected in his honour.

Heimdall became a cheerleader at American football matches, and got a job as a security officer at Microsoft.

Snorre, the unruly one, moved to USA and changed his name to Donald Trump.

Bjorn and Bjorn Again and Ulf became entertainers, and eventually won the Eurovision song contest as three quarters of a band called Abba.

Edward Bright was played by himself, or perhaps he was playing with himself?

Æthelred the Unready invented the battery.

Olaf the Pink Poof found a nice pretty boy called Julian Clary, and lived happily ever after in a pink cottage in Lavenham in Suffolk.

Eirik, Trygve, and Sigurd had a successful career appearing in many films as the three stooges.

The Valkyries became the one-hit wonders, known as Banananananaramaramarama.

And the bloke in kebab shop went into a business deal with Olaf Tryggvason. Olaf supplied Iceland burgers to his fast food chain, and he became a billionaire when he sold it to McDonald's in 1970.

Here endeth the full story of Maldon, 11th August, 991

The Nutivity 2014 (A gherkin birth)
(Written 24th/27th November, 2014)

In the deep mid-winter long, long, long ago,
Two unfortunate souls trudged through the ice and snow,
All the way from Kidderminster to Birminghem
with a cruel wind blowing in their faces,
To sign on for a job that paid the government minimum wage
on a zero hours contract basis.

Fairy Nuff and Pixie Snows were those simple folk. They loved each other, and had recently been married in a same sex gay ceremony by the vicar of Dudley. Pixie had wanted to make an honest woman of Fairy, because she knew that the love of her life wanted a baby, but as everybody knows it's not possible for two librarians to make a baby together. Not by normal means anyway.

But surprisingly Fairy had become stagnant, and so Pixie had to ask her, "Who's the daddy?"

Fairy told her the story that a few months before she had a mysterious and exciting vision.

She said," Do you remember that fellow called Ainsley Gaybloke we met on holiday in Caister last year?

Well, he appeared to me in a dream one night and performed a miracle with a turkey baster. And then he told me that I was carrying a very special baby boy for a very important reason. Then he said that the baby boy would be more famous than the Kidderminster Harriers centre forward who had scored 30 goals in the 2001/2002 season."

"Oh goodo!" replied Pixie, "I'm so glad that you didn't do the dirty deed with a man. Wow! It makes me feel sick just thinking about it."

It's a long way from Kidderminster to Birminghem, especially if you have to walk, and have no sense of direction. The two waifs had wandered around for days, going round in hopefully ever decreasing circles, passing through Rowley Regis, Blackheath, Selly Oak, and Edgbaston, before getting very confused. They were so confused that 2 days later they went round again through Rowley Regis, Blackheath, Selly Oak, and Bournville. The wind blew viciously through their thin Primark overcoats, and snow began to settle on the pavements of the bleak winter streets. So there they were, two refugees great with child, wandering the cruel streets of Birmingham cold and hungry, and desperate for work.

"It's beginning to look a lot like Smethwick, every where I go." Fairy sang sarcastically as she trudged on.

"Never mind!" said Pixie, "I know we're making some progress, 'cause I saw a sign to Aston back there. So we must be walking in a Villa hinterland."

When at last they arrived exhausted at the Bullring they found to their dismay that there was no room at the Premier Inn. But the bloke behind the reception desk was very kind.

"You's ladies are from Kidderminster aren't you?" he asked.

They both nodded.

Then he added, "I thought I recognised the accent. Tell you what, there's a bike shed round the back of the inn. Why don't you spend the night in there? "

They were so tired, and Fairy's time was drawing near, so they decided to take him up on his kind offer, even though they had to share their crude accommodation with 3 dickheads from Shepshed. They managed to scrounge £50 from Sir Bob Geldorf, who just happened to be passing by in his Rolls Royce on his way to a celebrity awards evening at the National Extradition Centre. So it was their good fortune that evening when they feasted on a slap up Indian meal at the nearby "Flaming Anus" tandoori restaurant. Then they settled down for a well earned sleep.

It was 3 o'clock in the morning when they were woken abruptly. A bright light shone like a star in the East. But it was only the West Midlands police helicopter with a massive searchlight. The 3 Shepshed Richards saw the bright light shining in the East as they washed their socks by night, and they were sore afraid. Everybody in the area knew that the helicopter cost an absolute bloody fortune to run, and that the local fuzz weren't very likely to fly around in it nonchalantly with any benevolent outlook. No, they had to nick someone otherwise the expense couldn't be justified. There had been a recent case where the fuzz had swooped down and arrested the whole family of Mustapha Shamani because he had committed two major crimes in the same week. First he was late back with his library book, "How to build an I.E.D in your garden shed", and then he had the brass faced Muslim cheek to park on a double yellow line outside the library. It was frontpage news when it was revealed that the Shamani family were being detained at the Guantanamo Bay detention camp.

Fairy Nuff wasn't feeling too well. She laid down flat on a kitchen table that had been dumped in the bike shed.

"I think that mutton vindaloo, the 9 onion bhajis, and the 5 pints of Kronenburg are laying a bit too heavy on me." she moaned.

Pixie was opening a large jar of cornichons she'd rescued from a skip outside the Co-op.

"Never mind, love!" she said," Try one of these little gherkins; they're delicious."

Fairy reluctantly nibbled on a cornichon, and to her surprise seconds later she gave birth to her baby boy, who she had been told by Ainsley Gaybloke to give the name Gee Whiz.

So Gee Whiz was born on a table in a bike shed in Birminghem. And Yes! It truly was a gherkin birth!

Suddenly all the bikes in the shed rang their bells in homage to the newborn, and the helicopter landed bringing 3 wise men. They were policemen, but they did bring gifts of pepper spray, handcuffs and warrants for everyone's arrest.

Music played in a house nearby as the helicopter took off and the snow continued to fall. It was a well known tune.

"And the boys from Birminghem City blues were singing "We love gays".".

And the sirens were screaming loud on Gee Whiz day.

Now we know the rest of the story, because Gee Whiz grew up to travel the land teaching people by telling them parabolas and one day he became the saviour of all mankind by rising to become the leader of UKIP.

The eyes follow you around the room
(Originally titled "The Painting")
(Written 20/27th January, 2014)

Lenny Davin put the phone down after saying, "I'm so grateful Lucas. Thank you so much. I'll be in touch soon."

He paced up and down, couldn't relax. It was a good job he had a huge spacious apartment otherwise he would have been in danger of wearing a long bare patch in the plush carpet. It was July, and air-conditioning was working at full blast, otherwise the sweltering New York weather, and traffic noise would have been unbearable. Lenny had lived in the Big Apple all his life and his swish warehouse apartment for over 15 years. He loved New York, its hustle and bustle, its orderly untidiness, its brutally different seasons, and its brash, get-out-of-my-way-I'm-too-busy-for-you attitude. As a celebrity photographer it had been good to him, brought him wealth and status. He had taken photographs of Presidents, Royalty, and major celebrities. At 65 he was in pretty good shape for native New Yorker.

He looked at his ornate clock a miniature version of the clock in Grand Central Station. It was 8. 05 pm. Half an hour that's all, and he would have the document that Lucas Protheroe had been putting together for him for more than 5 years. He had never been so nervous, so excited, so wound up like a coiled spring. He'd let the concierge know to bring the package straight up to number 174 when the motorcycle courier delivered it. Now all he could do was wait, and pace up and down, up and down wearing a groove in the carpet.

"Thirtyfive minutes! Where in the name of Sam Hill is that delivery boy?" he asked himself out loud, and then he went on, "Calm down! Calm down boy! You've waited for years, and a few minutes more won't make any difference."

Reassuring himself didn't stop him being on edge. He took a look out of the huge panoramic window, saw the traffic in the streets below snarling around in it's usual patterns, traffic lights on red and green, Walk and Don't Walk!, yellow cabs, delivery trucks, buses, 2 million people all moving with purpose in different directions.

"Ding Dong, Ding Dong!" the doorbell rang. His feet didn't touch the ground as he rushed across the room to open the door.

"Package for you Mr Davin." said the concierge handing over a big brown envelope.

"Thanks Johnny." he replied giving him the 5 dollar bill he'd been rolling around in his fist for nearly 40 minutes.

He sat down in his Bloomingdales luxury armchair, and breathed a big sigh. He looked at the package, and now he had it in his hand he wanted to savour the moment before opening it. It only took seconds to reflect the long road that he'd travelled to get to this moment in his life. He knew that some of what Protheroe had written for him would already be his common knowledge, but somewhere in amongst all of the ordinary stuff there would be some stones overturned with surprises lurking underneath. He began reading.

For the first 30 minutes it was all stuff he had imbedded in him like his own DNA. How his grandparents had emigrated to America from Florence, Italy in 1921, and arrived along with all the other hopefuls at Ellis Island Immigration Post looking for a better life. He remembered how his grandfather had told him all about the journey, for weeks getting to Hamburg in Germany and then across the Atlantic, and how thousands of people were quickly processed on arrival to be allowed into the New World. Papa Carlo, as he called him had told the story how many people left Europe with their real name and were quickly registered in America with a new truncated name. He was told about a friend he'd made on the voyage, who left Lithuania as Stanilaus Brzchinesvsky and discovered America as Stanley Birzin. Everybody had their names adulterated for the sake of efficiency and to meet the immigration clerks processing quotas.

The document Protheroe had produced illustrated the family line going further back through the generations. He had done a marvellous, precise and meticulously detailed job putting this work together. Lenny was getting deeper and deeper into his family tree. He studied each line carefully, where his ancestors lived in little villages like Anchiano around the City of Florence, births, christenings, marriages, deaths, occupations, through 20 generations. It took him hours as he pored over and absorbed every little detail. The task filled him with an overwhelming awareness of who he was and how he had come to be.

He was so immersed in his personal history he hardly noticed that 4 hours had dissolved as easily as cubes of sugar in his coffee cup. But the photographer felt he had to get to the crunch, the raison d'etre for all the expensive and time-consuming research that the best genealogist in America, if not the World, had done for him. And he wasn't just going to skip to the bottom line. No! He wanted to get there by savouring every moment, every nuance, and every little detail.

It was gone midnight. He took a deep breath, went to the kitchen and poured himself a beer, and then settled back down in the armchair. "Only 3 generations to go." he told himself.

An hour later and there it was. The proof! He grinned, and felt an electric pulse of extreme satisfaction move through him like a warm comfortable wave breaking on a sun-baked shore. It was confirmed. He was a direct descendant of the great man; some say the most intelligent man who has ever lived, the brilliant painter, sculptor, architect, musician, mathematician, engineer, inventor, anatomist, geologist, cartographer, botanist, and writer, Leonardo da Vinci. Lionardo di ser Piero da Vinci, born 15th April 1452 and died 2nd May 1519. Born out-of-wedlock, son of the wealthy Messer Piero Fruosino di Antonio da Vinci, a Florentine legal notary, and Caterina, a peasant girl.

That was what he wanted. That was what he had paid Protheroe to find out. Now he knew why he Lenny Davin was such a brilliant photographer. He shared some genes with his ancestor, an understanding of composition, light and shade, colour, shadow, foreground, background, expression. Delighted was not the word to describe where he was at that moment in time.

It was late, and he went to bed, fulfilled, ecstatic, feeling that the whole of his life had been leading up to that moment of discovery.

But he was exhausted after ploughing through the document. He didn't sleep well. The excitement of the previous few hours had his mind on a razor's edge, and soon his big windows were letting in the brightness of another New York day. He got up moving in a strange, floating way towards his armchair, and picked up the Protheroe document again. Maybe it was the lack of sleep, and his tired eyes, but he kicked himself because in his haste to open the envelope he had missed something the previous night. A large paperclip held another smaller envelope to the back of the family tree document that he had perused so carefully. On it Protheroe had written:

"My Dear Friend,

Don't open this until you are sure you want the whole truth.
This is dangerous stuff my friend!

Regards Lucas Protheroe"

Lenny felt sick. He went to the bathroom, and then into the kitchen to fix his breakfast, Columbian coffee, Florida orange juice, toast and Scottish marmalade. He wondered what that 2nd envelope would reveal. He switched on the massive flat screen TV, and tuned into a world news channel.

"Breaking news this morning from our news agency in Rome reports that the world famous genealogist Lucas Protheroe had been found dead in suspicious circumstances in his hotel room. He had been staying in the Hotel Palazzo Montemartini.

Mr Protheroe had been in Italy for nearly 3 years doing research work at many places in and around Florence, and in the Vatican archives. We'll update you on this report when we get more."

The New Yorker was stunned.

"What in the name of Sam Hill is going on?" he asked himself, and "What does Protheroe mean that this stuff is dangerous?"

His toast stuck in his gullet, his coffee didn't want to go down. He felt even more sick. He played with the envelope, turning it over and over in his trembling hands. He put it down , picked it up again, turned it over and over again, read the words on the front again 3 or 4 times.

"What can it be?" he asked himself, "It's not Pandora's box. It's just an envelope for Christ sakes."

He stared into space for a while trying to focus his mind on opening, or destroying, or maybe handing it over to the police.

"So Protheroe is dead! Maybe I owe it to him to find out why, if the clues are in this envelope." he told himself.

He steeled himself and slid his finger in the side to rip open the enclosure, took a deep breath and began reading.

"Oh Dear Lenny,
You are indeed a brave and possibly foolhardy man.
But my friend I have to tell you that no harm will come
to you if you stop reading now, and destroy what you
have in your hand. The consequences if you read on are
unpredictable, for you may have the future of America,
the World, and the human race in your hands."

This was Protheroe giving him a final chance, but Lenny had come this far and now he wasn't going to turn back. Something came back to him from his teenage years when he had heard a song called From the Underworld by a group called the Herd.

The lyric was based on a story from Greek mythology. He liked it so much he had committed it to memory. The words were ringing in his ears as his tortured mind told him to go and read on.

"Out of the land of shadows and darkness, we were returning towards the morning light,
Almost in reach of places I knew escaping the ghosts of Yesterday,
You were behind me following closely, "Don't turn around now" I heard you whisper in my ear,
"If you should turn now, all that you won will vanish just like a passing dream."

Just on the very verge of the morning, daylight was dawning; freedom was but a step away,
Now with the deep dark river behind us what could go wrong if I stayed strong in mind?
What was the sudden lapse into madness, what was the urge that turned my head around to look at you?
What was the stubborn will to destroy the love and the joy I nearly held?

Three times the thunder roared in my ears, in all of my years I'll see that lost look in your eyes,
As, with a sigh like smoke in the wind you slipped from my grasp into the waiting shadows,

So much I longed to say, but my touch found only the empty air and a black night's coldness,
Into another world you entered and never again I can reclaim you."

The song echoed around his brain distracting him from the task ahead. Then he took another deep breath, and read on. Protheroe had written:

"For five years I toiled away on this work for you, in the States, through Europe, and finally into Italy, and it was indeed a fascinating piece of research. In the end I had to get permission from the Vatican to research manuscripts hidden away since the early 1500's. Written in Latin at a time when most of the population were illiterate, Columbus had only just discovered America, and most scholars and theologians still believed the World was flat; this was painstaking work to analyse and interpret. But here goes. Brace yourself for a shock.

It was known that from September 1513 to 1516, under Pope Leo X, da Vinci spent much of his time living in the Belvedere in the Vatican in Rome. It was assumed that this was solely for him to undertake artistic projects for the Papacy, but I've discovered that isn't entirely true. The Papal Council were concerned that La Giaconda, better known nowadays as the Mona Lisa which it is claimed Leonardo painted between 1503 and 1507 illustrated some disturbing issues. The famous enigmatic smile being one, the way the eyes are set is another, but most worrying of all to the church elders was the background to the portrait which seemed to be "Of another World!"

In addition it was of concern to the authorities where their guest had acquired his engineering knowledge. He had designed bridges. In 1502 he produced a drawing of a single span 720-foot bridge as part of a civil engineering project for Ottoman Sultan Beyazid II of Constantinople. He had also drawn up plans for 2 flying machines, the helical rotor and the ornithopter.

So basically the High Church establishment were undermined and disturbed by his intelligence and how he had acquired it. They wanted to maintain a vice-like grip on all matters of knowledge or intelligence, and da Vinci was potentially a dangerous heretic. The manuscripts revealed evidence that while he was in the Belvedere he was tortured and eventually confessed that he had been abducted by aliens in May 1503, and had painted his most famous work

La Giaconda, the Mona Lisa, while on planet Zagafor 19, which is 37.2 light years from Earth

At the same time as Da Vinci had been stolen from the Earth the Zagafori had kidnapped a Florentine woman for the sole purpose of improving their bloodline. They became friends during their abduction and she is the subject of the painting of La Giaconda. Her smile reflects the exceptionally friendly treatment she was afforded by her alien captors. The background in the most famous painting in the World is other worldly because quite simply the artist and his sitter were both on another world when it was painted.

The aliens were super intelligent and highly advanced compared to their Earthly subjects. But at that time they were not hostile. In fact they enjoyed da Vinci's superior Earthly intellect, almost as much as they enjoyed the Florentine woman. Their male visitor was so trusted by them that that they allowed him access to their archives and libraries. So while the earthly genius was on Zagafor 19 he took the opportunity to study and copy the concepts he would employ for the Constantinople Bridge and the 2 flying machines. Despite his intellect he got them slightly wrong."

Lenny stopped reading at that point and reflected on what he had just learned. It was indeed an amazing and unbelievable revelation. But had he got to anything that could be marked as dangerous? It made him feel quite special that his ancient ancestor had been to another planet and consorted with aliens, and he fully understood why the Vatican wouldn't want this information to be common knowledge. It put the Catholic Church and the concept of One God on shaky foundations.

He read on.

"So now you know my friend that you are direct descendant of Leonardo da Vinci, and you know perhaps why he was such a brilliant and intelligent man. But his abduction has a sting in the tail, because the aliens only agreed to transport him and the woman back to Earth, and to allow the painting of the Mona Lisa to go back with them, with one certain very precise condition. And that was that from that point on in World history, starting with that masterpiece every painting subsequently produced would have eyes that seemed to follow the observer around the room. And the reason they do that my friend is that we are all being monitored. Those eyes are all like very advanced CCTV cameras.

WE ARE ALL BEING WATCHED BY MEN FROM OUTER SPACE, and when they feel the time is right for them they will come and get us.

In addition da Vinci learned that the Zagafori had throughout their history kidnapped species from other worlds, and assimilated their genes into their own bloodline. This was always a prelude to a benign invasion where the products of the species mixture would gradually take over the chosen planet. The gestation period for this plan to eventually populate the entire Universe was set as 1.3 treppia. This measurement was calculated by our Florentine mathematician as approximately 511.7 Earth years. Lenny, my friend, do the sums. 1503 add 511.7 years given a reasonable margin for error means that any day now............................"

Remember Road
(Written 22nd November, 2011)

Let me take you for a stroll down Remember Road,
and a walk across Nostalgia Square,
for a winding wander down Memory Lane,
to pick my forget-me-nots there.

Do you remember when Christmas didn't start in September, just after the Summer return, when Bonfire night was just one night, for everybody's big bang and big burn?,
We'd hardly heard of Halloween; there was no Trick or Treat,
and nobody needed to be frightened at night, when walking down the street.

Back in the days when Christmas came in December we had a real tree with candles to light.
There were strange smells like tangerines and chocolate, and they arrived on Christmas Eve night.
Back then, Christmas dinner was just chicken, and everyone enjoyed the sprouts (twice!),
and when I loosened a tooth on the sixpence in the Christmas pudding, the tooth fairy still came out.

When I was 6, I had my first taste of stardom, when I was in the school nativity play.
I was 1 of the 3 little shepherds, dressed in orange crepe paper outfits.
Suddenly, just before Jesus was born, the shepherds were standing in puddle,
after somebody accidentally pee'd themself on stage.
You've guessed it, Yes! It was me!

Let me take you for a stroll down Remember Road,
and a walk across Nostalgia Square,
for a winding wander down Memory Lane,
to pick my forget-me-nots there.

Do you recall when we all had to walk to school, and the cardboard in our shoes was getting wet, and
when there was free school milk in the morning, and school dinners were the best meal you'd get, and
when we learned our 12-times table from a blackboard, and went home covered in chalk dust?
Were you around when we had pounds, shillings and pence, and it made good sense to us?

Then you slept in a bed made with sheets and blankets, and if it was very cold, your Dad's overcoat as well.
We only had a fireplace in the living room. Do you remember that cosy glow and coal fire smell?
We still went to school in the winter snows, never mind the weather, and no matter what, and
you shared the bath water with the whole family, once a week whether you needed it or not.

Because I had 4 sisters, I always went into the bath last of all.
Well, I was outnumbered by them.
The water was cold and mucky by then, sometimes I came out more dirty than when I went in,
especially in the summer when I'd fallen in the river, that happened at least twice a week.
I always got the blame for the dirty ring around the bath, what a bloody cheek!

Let me take you for a stroll down Remember Road,
and a walk across Nostalgia Square,
for a winding wander down Memory Lane,
to pick my forget-me-nots there.

We might go scrumping for apples, play Knock down Ginger, or a million other pranks and tricks.
We'd go to Saturday Morning Pictures, or sneak into Woolworths to nick the pick-n-mix.
The Barbershop was in the back of Finlay's tobacconist; short back-and-sides the only choice,
because Sir might want "something for the weekend", women weren't allowed in with the boys.

What a treat it was to go Southend on a steam train; excitement rising as the sea drew near.
We had bags of chips, candyfloss, watched Punch and Judy, and walked to the end of the pier.
For hours long we played happily in the sewage outfall, and ate sandwiches made by Mum's fair hand.
Then went home contented, with seaweed between our toes, and pockets full of shells and sand.

Once a year we went to the Southend at night time, when they switched the illuminations on.
In those days there was a magical place, up on the cliffs called Never Never Land;
a fantasy land filled with fairy lights, and cartoon characters, and little waterfalls.
I loved it so much I wanted to live there, and often refused to go home.

Let me take you for a stroll down Remember Road,
and a walk across Nostalgia Square,
for a winding wander down Memory Lane,
to pick my forget-me-nots there.

There were so little traffic around in the street; you could safely play football, cricket, or tennis.
Indoors we played Ludo, Snakes and Ladders, Tiddlywinks; we were Beryl the Peril, or Dennis the Menace.

We all had manners, said please and thank you, excuse me, and I'm sorry, and all with a smile.
And Father Christmas didn't have to be CRB checked, to make sure he wasn't a paedophile.

On Sundays, we listened to the radio; there was Family Favourites, and the Billy Cotton Band Show.
On the monochrome 9 inch telly we watched Robin Hood, and Roger Moore was Ivanhoe.
The whole house was filled with a lovely smell, as Mum baked cakes in the afternoon,
and all us kids hung around expectantly, and argued about who was going to lick the bowl.

So its certain my friends, that life was surely much simpler then, even if our table was bare.
There were no CDs, or DVDs, or LCD TVs, no IPODs, or mobile phones back there.
We communicated by stopping and talking face to face, everyone had time to listen.
There was a gazunder under the bed, we were lucky 'cause we did have a pot to piss in.

There was no Facebook, No Twitter, No Email, No Internet, No XBOX, No Ebay, no Google, and certainly no pot noodle.
And no political correctness, Thank God!
There was No money, scruffy clothes, no cars, a snotty nose, no sweets, not very much too eat,
but there was lots of love, and lots of fun, and smiles from everyone.

Well we went for a stroll down Remember Road,
and a walk across Nostalgia Square,
for a winding wander down Memory Lane,
to pick my forget-me-nots there.

Have you seen the latest newscast?
(Written 6th May, 2015)

"I was eavesdropping when I heard." said 102J11.

"Really! Where were you?" replied 709A15.

"In the Nutrition Station at Government House 47."

709 laughed.

"Well normally I would tell you not to believe everything you hear, but in this case I'm very happy to tell you it's true."

"You're happy? But it's terrible news, and I'm not sure I'm going to be able to follow the new regulations."

"Listen 102; you are very young and you don't have the benefit of living through the last 2 centuries like I have. I can tell you with great certainty that if the Emperor says it's right then it is."

"But why are you so sure? Doesn't our administration make mistakes?" said 102 with frustration.

709 smiled and began to explain.

"Look!" he said, "Let me go through the history."

"OK, if you must." 102 responded.

709 was very fond of repeating the history.

102 just expected it was what old people did.

"When the Emperor took over we were in a real mess. The world was in financial turmoil, and all our care systems were becoming entropic. We were heading for a global revolution taking us into the abyss. Terrorism, Nationalism, Separatism, arguments over climate change, religious bigotry, increasingly violent food riots, were all prominent, and those were only the tip of the iceberg.

The Emperor was elected legitimately by the people, and within 10 years enormous strides were made. Not only did he sort out our national status, our place in the world, our absolute global financial superiority, our immigration policy;" he paused, "Need I go on?"

102 knew that when 709 got into his stride there was no stopping him. So he just decided that a reply would be futile.

The elder 709 continued.

"When the administration came up after 12 years with a cure for all cancers, then all known diseases, and then ultimately a cure for aging and death itself, how could we not believe in our beloved leader? It goes without saying that having got us out of the European Community his master stroke was to keep the Cure All exclusively for the English people. He'd succeeded only months before in breaking up the UK and devolving our satellite nations; those hangers-on in Scotland, Wales and Northern Ireland. So we didn't have to look after all those whining parasitic spongers anymore. No! Now we were back on our own; masters of our own destiny."

709 stopped and smiled at his companion, giving the look that said "You can speak now."

102 stroked his chin, and thoughtfully offered, "I don't believe that it was just a lucky coincidence that first our great leader kept the Cure All available only in England, and then that global virus of 2029 just killed off everybody else on the planet. I think the administration developed a sort of antidote to the Cure All, and spread it around the planet."

"Don't you see?" said 709 getting more heated, "It really doesn't matter anyway. Who cares about all those Krauts and Dagos, and Wops, and Chinkies, and Yanks, and all the fucking Moslem troublemakers? Did we need to give a shit about whether Scotland had been renamed Nicolandia, and all their stupid claims to our oil? Whether it's coincidence or not, it was just brilliant, because it left us in charge again. Once again Britannia, or should I say Englandia ruled the waves, and this time there were no inferior races to upset the applecart. It was our world. We were the Gods."

"It wasn't Britannia though was it, or even Englandia?"

"OK, I stand corrected. I accept that when we repopulated the rest of that thankfully empty world the Emperor had renamed our nation as Greater Faragia. But didn't he deserve to have it all named after him after all the administration's achievements?"

102 sighed.

"OK, so I accept your version of history as an explanation of how we got where we are today, but I still can't believe that the Emperor is going to reverse the State Programme for Enforcement of Reproduction Management, and that is what I heard sitting here just a few minutes ago."

"My friend, how old are you now?"

"I'm 25 next birthday. Why do you ask?"

"Well, due to the administration's wonderful medical advances, I am now approaching my 179th birthday. I had my Cure All when I was 32 and that is why I look so young today. But because I am ancient in years, unlike you I can remember the old ways before the unfortunately named SPERM policy was brought in. Nowadays, in the year of our Emperor 150, which translates back on my old calendar as 2165 AD, the SPERM policy separates the 2 human impulses of sexual gratification and reproduction of the species into 2 diverse functions. What that does is 2 things. First, it makes it possible to contain population growth by grooming our offspring in a laboratory given the necessary government approval. There's a neat bi-product in that our female citizens no longer have to go through the pain and distress of childbirth, and obviously there are no longer any unwanted pregnancies like in the bad old days. Secondly, all any adult needs to do to acquire a pseudo-orgasm whenever and wherever that is desired, is to take a little pill and wait 10 minutes. Now, I know that all sounds brilliant to you youngsters, but I can tell you that reverting back to the old ways, although it has some risks, is so much more fun."

"I'm not convinced," replied 102, "When we had our relationship counselling back in Educational Training they showed us something horrible called pornography, where people were doing something physical just for pleasure and not for making babies, and it looked very energetic, extremely time-consuming and not to say very messy and unhygienic. To me it looks totally disgusting, all that pushing and shoving, and heavy breathing. I'm not at all sure that I'm going to like having to do it that way when the new law comes in."

"Oh please, trust me 102, you will, you will!"

Don't Talk to Me about Gherkins
(Written 12th July, 2016)

There's a wise old man called Ernie,
who lives down by the Maylandsea shore.
He's been growing a beard to hide his face,
for fifty years or more.
I think he's an octogenarian,
perhaps he's the old man of the sea,
I think he harbours a secret,
he's concealing from you and from me.
I asked him once what his secret was,
to keeping his old heart working.
He looked at me through his wise old eyes, and said,
"Don't talk to me about gherkins."

Ernie'll talk to you about anything you like,
about politics, religion and sex.
He'll argue with you 'til you're black and blue,
and get you all heated and vexed.
He'll talk about the sky, and apple pies and DIY,
and natter on about any matter you don't understand.
He'll waffle and procrastinate, pontificate and quietly debate,
on any subject that accidentally comes to hand.
His knowledge is as long as his beard,
and his beard would rival Rasputin's,
but he draws the line and calls time by saying,
"Don't talk to me about gherkins."

Ernie was hungry and went down to the chippie
to buy a ton of chips and a wing of skate.
He'd been working hard in the garden all day,
and he wasn't pleased to have to wait.
His hunger grew as he stood in the queue;
his appetite came in on a trolley.
He asked the lovely chip shop girl,
"Could you throw me in a wally?"
She said "Sorry! Ain't got none of them."
He said, "Really! What's in that big jar a-lurking?"
She said, "Oh them are pickled cucumbers."
He said, "Don't talk to me about gherkins."

Research for this poem didn't come easy, that's for sure,
but after all, that's what I've got a rhyming dictionary for.
There's really only two words
that have a perfect rhyme with gherkin.
First, there's an old fashioned measure of liquid
that once was called a firkin,
and last there's an interesting word,
I'd never heard of before, and
it's something called a merkin.
It's a device to hide your modesty
like Adam and Eve's leaves of figs,
A merkin my dears,
now I know you are all ears,
is a decorative pubic wig.
So merkin, firkin, gherkin, and that's your lot,
I'm really sad to have to tell.
Please don't talk to me about hairy merkins,
and it would be best to avoid discussion
about firkin gherkins as well.

Ernie's seen a lot of changes over the years;
The world keeps spinning and none of us will last.
One thing that's definitely not good,
is the emergence of food that's fast.
Ronald McDonald lives everywhere,
from rising moon to setting sun,
and nobody knows why his Big Macs
have a gherkin in the burger bun.
I think it would be very apt and not absurd,
when Ernie croaks and has his last laugh,
that he have carved on his gravestone in bold letters,
"Don't talk to me about gherkins."
Yes! That's his epitaph.

Diversions
(Written 15th September, 2014)

"God! I hate airports." he muttered to himself as he pulled into the car park at Stansted. The Ferrari purred to a halt, and Ryan Cousins stepped out, glad that the short trip from Chelmsford through the miserable, continuous drizzle of the September early evening rain was over. He was excited. Simone Taylor, his unbelievably gorgeous Simone, was coming home early.

It had been an unexpected strange text that reached his mobile that afternoon while he was still at work. He had planned to be making an arduous, boring, journey around the M25 to Heathrow the next afternoon in the busiest time of the day. But a few hours ago out of the blue he'd received a text which said "Hi lovely Sugarman, Flight from Miami rescheduled. Arriving Stansted on American Airlines AMA 3982X landing at 19:30 today. Love you loads. XXX Your sweet Monkeychild XXX."

Ryan didn't mind; because his beautiful, supermodel girlfriend would be back in his bed a whole 24 hours earlier than expected. He felt horny just at the thought of what he would do to her, or was it what she would do to him, once they were together in the sack? And, there was a big bonus. Stansted was only 30 minutes easy drive away, and fairly civilised; at least compared to the organised bedlam of Heathrow, negotiated around the intermittent car park of the M25.

Ryan made his way from the car park to the arrivals hall, queued up for an Americano black coffee, bought himself an "Evo" car magazine, and settled down within view of the information screen. About 15 minutes later there it was on the screen. "AMA 3982X landed on time"

He took a deep breath, and his heart skipped 3 beats as he merged into the excited huddle of people waiting for the arrivals. He knew that he could have waited until the screen said "AMA 3982X in baggage reclaim", but the thought of seeing Simone again overwhelmed him with a delightful impatience. His thoughts focussed on her and only her.

She had been away for 3 long weeks on a modelling assignment in Miami and the Florida Keys. Oh boy! Had he missed her. All those nights indoors alone talking to himself, feeling like he'd been abandoned, and then filling time by organising going out with the boys to have a few beers and talk football. Well, it just wasn't what he really wanted.

He wanted her. He wanted to ogle greedily at her curves, run his hands over her delicious bare skin, and look into her deep green eyes and see that look that told him everything he wanted to know. He wanted to smell her perfume, breathe in the summer meadows in her long blonde hair, nibble her ear, and tell her sweet nothings. He wanted to wake up with her there, blonde locks spilling onto the pillow, her body gently rising and falling with each soft and gentle breath. He wanted that smile when she woke up and saw him laying there adoring her.

Now the waiting was over! There she was! Strutting that confident supermodel strut, pink and purple designer Gucci luggage being carried by a porter. Ryan waved. Simone smiled. They met.

He swung her around in his arms and kissed her passionately.

"Wow! You look gorgeous, my darling, I've missed you so much." he said, never letting his gaze move from her eyes. Her perfume didn't smell quite how he had been imagining it moments before, but he thought that 7 or 8 hours cocooned in the air-conditioned prison of a 767 might have something to do with that.

"I've missed you too, Sugarman." she smiled back. He noticed that her voice was different too; not quite like her velvety smooth, chocolate ice-cream tones, but a more rasping, rough-edged hue. He knew that she always smoked too much when she was away on a modelling assignment. She had told him many times in the past that it might all look glamorous and exciting, but modelling was really hard work.

They started the short walk to the car park holding hands, while the porter followed diligently.

"I'm so tired," she said, "It's been a gruelling 3 weeks. Would you mind, darling, if we skip the travelogue for now? What I need at the moment is to have a nap while you take me home."

He thought that was odd. She was usually bursting with excitement whenever she returned from an assignment, wanting to tell all about every little detail of the exotic places she'd travelled to, and been photographed in.

He replied, with concern, "OK. If that's what you want, my little Monkeychild. We'll be home soon, and then you can relax and tell me all about it."

She smiled a thin smile, and said nothing. Ryan paid the porter and squeezed the posh luggage into the Ferrari, and then opened the passenger door for Simone. She climbed in, reclined the seat, and was snuggling in the land of nod before he'd strolled round to the driver's side and started the engine.

There had been no let up in the pattern of autumn drizzle. The Ferrari glided through the evening's early darkness as the couple made their way homeward along the fast and efficient dual carriageway of the A120. He focussed on the road, with the occasional glance to his left, thinking again about how wonderful it would be when he got home with his prize. He imagined them having a long, lazy bath together, drinking bucks fizz, and chatting about her time away, before going to bed, and renewing their closeness in the most passionate and exciting way.

The lady who sat next to him was somewhere else light years away.

They turned off the main road near Dunmow and joined the Chelmsford Road winding down through Barnston village. The drizzle turned to an angry squall and the tall trees at the sides of the country road swayed erratically in the sudden wind, which heralded the onset of a thunder storm. The windscreen wipers were working overtime, and it was one of those nights when the normally very effective headlights seemed to have trouble showing the road ahead with any clarity. These driving conditions were dangerous and Ryan wasn't about to take any risks. He eased off the gas. Slowly but surely they eased their way past the villages of Onslow Green and North End.

The passenger stirred a little in her seat while crosswinds buffeted the Ferrari, but she didn't say anything. Suddenly the driver could see blue flashing lights ahead, and then a workman in a high-vis jacket stood in the middle of the road waving the Ferrari down.

"What's the trouble, Officer?" asked Ryan.

"Road's flooded ahead, and there's been a four car pile up near Hartford End." the man replied.

"Bloody awful night. Anybody hurt?"

"Yeah, 3 fatalities, and 2 people in a bad way. Ambulances on the way."

Ryan felt a stab of apprehension at continuing the journey.

"Oh that's terrible," he sympathised, "At least Broomfield Hospital's not far away."

"Where you headed, Sir?"

"Chelmsford, Writtle, near the green."

"Take the next on the right down through Pleshey and then follow the road through Chignall St James. It'll bring you out on the Roxwell Road side of the city."

"OK, thanks."

"Goodnight, Sir, drive safely."

Ryan turned off towards Ringtail Green. He drove slowly. He didn't know the road at all. The weather worsened. The country lane was more like a stream, and each of the gaps between the lightning and the thunder was only two heartbeats. He seriously thought about turning back and taking refuge in the Butcher's Arms until the storm was over. He looked at Simone, still asleep, and thought, "No. We'll be home soon, if I drive slowly and carefully. She deserves to be looked after. I have to get her home."

There was a sharp bend to the right near Dropshots, and as he turned the wheel there was a flash of lightning, and an ear-splitting crash of thunder like someone had dropped a grenade on the car. Luckily, he had been crawling along, at less than 20 miles an hour. So he managed to bring the car to a halt in time.

At first, it looked like a crumpled soggy bundle of dark clothing in the middle of the road, but the lightning soon showed it was a large man dressed in a black coat and wearing a trilby hat. Ryan put the headlights on full beam, and a few yards from where the man lay motionless he could see ahead there was a dark blue van at right angles blocking the road.

"What do I do now?" he asked himself. Simone hadn't stirred, but his first thoughts were to protect her.

He got out of the car, and was drenched in an instant. His eyes filled with rain, and his smart grey suit suddenly hung on his body like a heavyweight diver's outfit. He locked the car, and walked over to the casualty.

There was another fork of lightning as he approached the body and bent down.

"Are you all right, my friend?" he enquired.

The bundle of clothes groaned, rolled over to face him, and looked him straight in his water-filled eyes.

He was shocked. It was Colin Johnson, his old adversary from the days when he had been setting up his construction business 5 years ago. In an instant, the blue van's doors burst open, and two men dressed head to toe in black, leapt out and grabbed him from behind, roughly forcing his arms down by his sides. The dark bundle eased slowly up from the tarmac, and snarled "Hello, Ryan, fancy meeting you here."

In the next lightning flash Ryan saw the rapid movement of a long steel blade in Colin's right hand. He squealed as the point came rushing in under his ribs on his left side, and was then turned and twisted slowly and agonisingly, as a red warm stream of blood squirted out of his body. His attacker grinned at the enjoyment of his vengeance. The victim gasped his last breath, and as it abandoned his lungs like a whisper in a distant misty void, he thought he saw her through the reddening rain, smiling. It wasn't the smile that he craved, that Simone smile that told him everything he wanted to know. It was a wicked, malevolent smile.

The next day American Airlines flight number AMA 3983 landed at Heathrow early, at 18:30. Simone, the supermodel, didn't understand when Ryan, the love of her life, the only man she had ever loved, wasn't at the airport to meet her.

Thank You. No!
(Written 1st June, 2014)

While I've been away from home, my space has been invaded by a pernicious little character called the postman. He understands that my weak spot is a little flap in my front door called the letter box, and he has no hesitation in making almost daily use of it.

So when I return home, there on my doorstep are the results of the postman's endeavours. Sometimes, seldom in fact, his deposits on my mat are good news. Most of the time, if they have any true relevance to my life, they are bills illustrating that I owe money to some organisation. Strangely. I don't really mind any of that. But what does irritate me is the other stuff.

Leaflets! Piles of bloody leaflets, every bloody day.

Do I want a pizza-to-go, from Domino?

Do I want a takeaway curry from yet another new Indian restaurant that's recently taken over another ailing pub?

Do I want a different broadband provider, like TalkTalk or PlusNet, and why do BT bombard me with information about fibre optics when I'm clearly quite happy with my copper wire wi-fi?

Do I have any need of yet more insurance from Direct Line, or some company that wants to bet me that I'm going to die, but in the process of getting there, is convinced that I'll just quietly hand over a wodge of cash to them?

How does the double glazing company not know that I might live in a cave, and don't have any windows?

Does the solar panel company know that caves don't have roofs?

Why does every bank want to offer me another credit card with an extortionate APR?

Why does MY BANK not check their records before they offer me a credit card that I already have?

Why do Saga think that I can afford to go on one of their cruise holidays costing £4,000?

There is only one answer to these invasions of my space.

Straight in the recycling bin is where they go, with a very polite, and restrained, Thank You. No!

While I'm at home, there's a very clever technical device that has a persuasive grasp on my attention. It sits in the corner and lures me daily to pay homage. Some of the time the TV is interesting and educational, but increasingly it has become a hole in the world that serves up continuous crap. I often ask myself was it better when we only had 5 channels, of even 2?

Now we've got hundreds of channels all serving up the TV equivalent of MacDonald's Big Mac and Fries.

Who in their right mind watches "Big Brother"?

How many times do we all want to see people eating cockroaches on "I'm a Celebrity, pay me loads of money.", and I'll sit in the jungle being obnoxious for 2 weeks, while being starved, and surrounded by rats and spiders.

Why is everybody on "Eastenders" so bloody miserable? Real Eastenders are cheerful and worldly-wise; if not intelligent.

When did "Emmerdale" morph from a wholesome story about farms, sheep, and bread making, into a sordid tale of bed hopping, cheating, and subterfuge?

How long will it be before I'm selected to be yet another obnoxious contestant on "Come Dine with Me"?

Why is it that every bed and breakfast establishment on "Four in a Bed" thinks it's reasonable to charge £200 a night, sometimes without breakfast?

Why is the weather forecast always more wrong on BBC?

Why don't they apologise when they so persistently get it wrong.

When will one of the programmes featuring people getting drunk on a Saturday night, fighting in the streets, and peeing and puking up in any available corner, come to Chelmsford?

Is it a fact that I've already seen all the movies that are worth watching several times? Can it be that there really is nothing new to show me but more gruesome violence, more explicit sex, and more car chases, and all constructed with CGI?

Do I want to watch "About a Boy", "My Beautiful Launderette", or "Carry on Osama bin Laden" again and again and again?

I know who shot J.R. and I know who killed Tina in "Coronation Street", but who murdered Bruce Forsyth and replaced him with a hologram?

So most of the time TV is just background noise like a placebo to fill the silence. Do I watch it much?

Thank You. No!

Ah but isn't it distressing to find to find that sometimes, only sometimes, the TV advertisements are better than the programmes? That doesn't apply all the time of course.

Why do Virgin and Sky spend so much money trying to persuade me to subscribe to their TV systems? Surely a fair proportion of the people watching are already using them.

Why is it that if I send £2 to Africa they can have fresh water, when it costs me about £300 a year?

Why do I need a Stannah Stairlift when I live in a cave, and don't have stairs?

If Ian Botham goes for a walk so often, why does he need Revitive?

Why don't all the football referees at Chelmsford City's matches go to Specsavers?

Has Michael Parkinson got life insurance from the company he wants me to subscribe to?

How many mistreated donkeys are there being illegally imported into Britain? Will they take our jobs, and nick our women?

Has Britain been secretly invaded by UKIP voting Russian immigrant meerkats?

Why do they keep showing me starving children in Africa just as I'm sitting down to eat?

Why don't the governments of the countries in Africa, where the children are starving, feed their people, instead of buying guns and mining for uranium?

Do I take any notice of the adverts? Obviously I do, otherwise I wouldn't have said come up with this diatribe. But do I buy any of the products advertised? Thank You. No!

So you've probably guessed by now, that my favourite TV programme is "Grumpy Old Men", and I don't have much sentiment for being treated like an idiot, or being regarded as a soft touch for any old charity.

The milk of human kindness has soured in the jug.

The sweet taste of charity has vanished in the fug.

I'm a product of the media, an average man in the street,
but most of all I'd like to think I'm nobody's mug.

So to all that modern chewing gum, throw away after use, disposable disposables world I say,

Thank You. No!

Thank You. No!

And that's all I've got to say.

Angel's Mission
(Written 24th December, 2014 to 5th January, 2015)

Somehow that Christmas was always destined to be different. Just like every other Christmas we had spent weeks before enjoying our time helping Santa and the elves getting all the children's presents ready, streamlining Santa's sleigh, and polishing Rudolph and the other reindeers noses. We had the usual deadline to meet and everything had to be ready on Christmas Eve.

I think I've said before now that I've spent a very long, time training to be an angel, and enjoying every minute of it. I remember long ago starting with simple things like sewing crystals made from raindrops on the edges of clouds so that they would all have a silver lining. Then I spent some time knitting sunbeams together in the right order to make rainbows, and making sure that they were positioned not to touch the ground, so that there was no need to hide a pot of gold at each end. Eventually I progressed to making clouds; every possible kind, from great big towering cumulonimbus to delicate feather-like cirrus, and big dramatic storm clouds with their frightening thunder and lightning. I'd often be sitting with my angel friends on a favourite cloud playing my golden harp, and winding harp strings from angel hair, and we sometimes invented new colour shades for our skies to help us paint precious gold sunsets blazing day's glorious end. As always, some of my very favourite nights were spent catching falling stars, and putting them in my pocket, and saving them for a rainy day. Gabriel had given me a special purple pouch to put my falling stars in, so that they would never fade away. They were very special because when I needed them I could use them to perform magical deeds.

That Christmas Eve, as I was taking a little rest idly swinging on a star after a hard day's work, I was asked to go and see Gabriel again. He told me that he was continually delighted with my progress, and that very soon I would go with my friend Sebastian on a special mission. He said that he knew how rewarding I found guardian angel duty, and gently reminded me that it was all about looking after people who needed a bit of help, maybe sitting over someone's shoulder, and whispering to them to save them from harm or danger. He said that when I'd gone on my last angel's holiday and so skilfully used that crashing aeroplane as a timely distraction to work my magic deeds; it had brought a tear to his eye and a lump to his throat.

"What is this special mission?" I asked Gabriel, "And what will I be doing?"

He just smiled at me and said it was a great honour to be selected and I'd have to wait and see, because special missions always needed at least two experienced angels to work out what to do for the best. He couldn't tell me where I would be going; just that it would be very soon.

I went back to my duties.

I was carrying some moonbeams home in a jar, wondering what my special mission would be, when I bumped into my old friend Sebastian and he told me how excited he was to be going with me.

He knew that unlike a holiday a special mission would be much more difficult, and that it was a big test only allocated to experienced angels. But he also advised me that we had to be very, very careful because there were always consequences.

Then he said with a broad smile "We'll be fine my friend, if we do the right thing!"

Just like before when I'd gone on my holiday, I found when I tried to sleep that night I was nervous and excited. I kept waking up with very loud and disturbing noises ringing in my ears and each time my eyes were blinded by flashes of the brightest light. The noises and flashes of light were louder, brighter, and more violent and insistent than the thunder and lightning of the biggest thunderstorm I'd ever helped to roll together.

The next morning when I woke up, I wasn't on my beautiful cloud with a silver lining, sewn by my own fair hand. I was in a very different place; a trench with a lot of very cold and distressed men wearing mud splattered khaki uniforms. They were eating cold food out of tins and smoking endless cigarettes. I was wearing the same uniform, and my feet were ankle-deep in squelching mud. Every now and then, the leader, who carried a stick and wore a slightly different uniform with a leather flat hat blew a whistle, and then there would be a lot of shouting, and the noises and flashes I'd heard and seen earlier would start again from another trench about 200 yards away. The ground shook with every explosion, the noises were ringing in my ears, and smoke billowed up and filled my lungs with choking, acrid, dirty air. Some men climbed out of the top of the trench and ran towards the noises firing their rifles and throwing grenades. There were screams and shouts and lots of very bad language. Most of the men were never seen again, but those who managed to crawl back terrified to the comparative safety of the trench were covered in mud and blood. Sometimes they dragged back badly injured comrades with fingers, hands, feet, or even arms and legs missing.

It was very cold; snow was falling all the time. There were only three colours to be seen in this hellhole; shades of khaki and brown for uniforms and mud, white snow in the skies and collecting in holes in the ground, and red blood running in rivulets in every groove of the ground, and often in the wrinkles of the men's faces. There was an awful burnt, charred, sickly smell.

As suddenly as the commotion had begun, it stopped, and the whole world seemed to breathe a sigh of relief. But big, tough looking men were crying like babies, injured men were screaming in agony, dying men were stuttering their last prayers. There was very little anyone could do to help. I was very afraid.

A man next to me leaned against the back of the trench, lit a cigarette, and turned to look at me. He had fear in his bloodshot weary eyes, and his face was contorted as he cried and issued some despairing words.

"They told us it would be over by Christmas, and all us brave boys would be going home as heroes. We're fighting for king and country, they said. What do they know?"

We sat there for a while in the despair and desolation, only waiting for the next whistle to spring us into another futile action. The snow began to pile up in the hollows in the ground, and there was a rush of icy chill which cut right through me, and then the leader in the leather hat hit me with his stick and shouted at me, "Oy! New boy! Go with the work detail to collect the dead bodies. Hold up this Red Cross flag and if you're lucky the bastards over there might not shoot you."

He had a stern, grim face and he ushered me over the top of the trench into the cold unrelenting wind of no-man's land, and pointed me towards the opposite trench. As I climbed nervously over the top something very strange happened. All the men started singing.

"God save our gracious king, long live our noble king, God save our king....."

It sounded very out of place in this hell on Earth.

I stumbled forward in a daze, edging my way through the freezing mud and depressions filled with snow, barbed wire, discarded weapons and hats, bits of bodies, peering through the snow with smoke and the stench of death in my nostrils. As I negotiated my way expecting to be felled by machine gun fire any moment, I thought I saw another man with a Red Cross flag moving towards me from the enemy trench. He was wearing a different uniform. It was a funny shade of darkish green, with a thin red band around his hat. Then another strange thing happened. From the trench in front of me I heard more singing, almost like a protesting chant of the singing behind me.

"Deutschland, Deutschland uber alles, uber alles in der Weldt....."

As the other man with the flag drew closer, I thought I recognised him. No! My eyes were playing tricks with me. Surely not! It can't be! We were only a few steps away from each other. A familiar smile, a hand offered in friendship. I clasped the hand and shook it with all my compassion.

"Sebastian! Sebastian! My dear friend, I am so glad to see you." I spluttered.

"Hello, Michael. I'm so pleased you are here. We have work to do. Are you ready?" my fellow angel replied.

Instinctively we pulled our purple pouches from our pockets.

"You know what to do, don't you?" Sebastian said. I nodded and we set off in opposite directions, scattering handfuls of our collected falling stars from the pouches into the air, up and down the unholy area of no-man's land. They floated in the misty, snow filled atmosphere twinkling in gentle flickering snowflakes and slowly glided down to the mud beneath our feet. After a while, when our pouches had been emptied, the ground was aglow with a strange translucent green light which seemed to swirl like a ghostly whirlpool. The singing from either side had stopped, and we could see candles being lit and the eyes of men peering over the tops of the trenches in curiosity.

Suddenly, there was singing again, but not the patriotic, divisive words of earlier. Behind me they sang, "Silent night, holy night, all is calm, all is bright........"

In front of me they sang, "Stille Nacht, heilige Nacht, Alles schläft; einsam wacht......"

But they sang, in harmony, beautifully, the same tune, but different words.

Sebastian and I just stood there smiling at each other. Over and over again the song echoed out across the field we had been preparing. And then just before dawn the song ended with a collective triumphant chorus.

From one side they concluded with, "Jesus, Lord, at Thy birth, Jesus, Lord, at Thy birth."

And from the other, "Christ, in deiner Geburt! Christ, in deiner Geburt!"

There was a pause, like the whole world was standing still for a moment and then a stream of a million blindingly bright twinkling stars, curved in a magnificent continuous lightshow, making their way in a glorious triumphant free ribbon up into the fast fading blackness of the heavens.

We spontaneously hugged each other, and as we did this, men began climbing out of the opposite trenches running towards us, shouting "Merry Christmas!" and " Fröhliche Weihnachten!"

Soon we were surrounded by men from both sides, shaking hands, smiling, laughing, and swapping cigarettes and sweets. The bright twinkling stars swirled the magnificent lightshow around all of us, seeming to wrap us in a huge sense of relief and joy. Then the men formed a circle around Sebastian and me, and each man took a snow ball out of his pocket, and with a tumultuous shout of," Hurrah! Hurrah! Hurrah!" threw the snowballs in the air above our heads. We ducked, both expecting to be hit by an avalanche of wet snow. Then there was another long silence, as if the whole Universe was taking a deep breath, followed by a huge flash of blinding light. Everybody flattened themselves quickly on the ground thinking the hostilities had begun again, but when they dared to look up; out of the new dawn light a football fell to the ground. Sebastian got to his feet and kicked the football in the air, and that signalled the start of a kick about.

Some men threw down their coats for makeshift goals, and Tommies United were playing Hermann Athletic with one hundred men a side and nobody counting the goals scored. In a strange ironic twist the Tommies' goalkeeper was Werner Karlsblatt, a butcher from Wiesbaden, and the Hermann's top scorer was Sidney Whitehouse, a blacksmith from Redditch, and nobody was in the least bit worried about that.

"We've done a good job here, Sebastian." I smiled at my angel comrade, as the game continued around us.

"Indeed we have, Michael, my friend." he replied.

We stood in what would have been the centre circle of the makeshift football pitch very pleased with ourselves, as the ball came flying through the air towards us. We both jumped up to head the ball, cracked heads, and fell to the floor knocked out.

When I opened my eyes I was back on my favourite cloud, and Sebastian was sitting next to me.

"We did the right thing, my friend." he smiled," Or we wouldn't be back here now"

And with that we carried on catching falling stars and putting them in our pockets, and saving them for a rainy day. A few days later we were back on the cloud talking about our special mission when Gabriel turned up.

"I am so pleased with you, Michael and Sebastian, "he said, "Christmas was different for those men this year, but you do need to know that sadly the next day the fighting resumed."

"So what was the point then?" I asked, feeling a little confused.

"Ah, well," Gabriel explained," You see, it's a fact that sooner or later all the men there that day will die, if not in battle, then after the war is over. That's just the way life is."

"Yes, I know that," I said, "But that doesn't explain why we went."

Gabriel sighed, "My friend, you still have much to learn."

He paused, and his face broke into gentle smile, "Michael!" he said, "Because of the work that you and Sebastian did on that Christmas day, every man there will benefit. Whether they died as enemies on the battlefield, or carried their awful memories of the conflict into old age, when they reach Heaven they will all be friends."

Courgette (The story of Cheryl and Pete)
(Written 21st October, 2014)

She was a cheeky, curvaceous
and charming courgette,
looking for love on the Internet;
gorgeous and green, and obviously willing,
were her admirable credentials,
and a good sense of humour in her beau,
were her vegetable essentials.

But the trawl through the trash
on the websites for dating
just made her despair
for that longed-for perfect mating.
She was plagued with no-hopers,
in all shapes and sizes;
A motley crew, but
what can you do with vegetables
that don't win prizes?

Cauliflowers from Carlisle,
and a sweet potatoes from Peru,
curly kale from Skelmersdale,
and tomatoes, and shoots of bamboo,
bok choy and choi sum,
mustard greens and parsnips,
artichokes from Jerusalem,
and soyabeans and turnips,

lettuces from Latvia,
and kohlrabi from Tehran,
some mange tout from Montpelier,
an aubergine from the Sudan.

There was broccoli and endives,
and radishes and beets,
brussels sprouts and asparagus,
and a few shallots and leeks,
mustard greens from the Philippines,
carrots, celery, and okra,
onions, spinach, parsnips, garlic,
mung beans and alfalfa,
cucumbers from Chicago,
peppers and avocados,
chard, mooli and collard greens,
watercress and green beans.

A sadness descended upon her, and
she began to weep and to howl.
Her search had gone on far too long.
She was just about to throw in the trowel.
And then she found the perfect match,
a pumpkin boy from Plaistow.
Her joy was overwhelming
when she found her love at last, oh!

They were married in Malibu
in a mad whirlwind romance,
and honeymooned in Heaven
in a lovely chateau in France.
They set up home in Norfolk,
in a semi in Kings Lynn,
and later that year they were proud to be
the parents of zucchini twins.

The Guitarist
(Written 9th April, 2015)

Underneath the stairs in a small alcove in the hall the piano laid gathering dust, unloved and un-played, even at Christmas. In the un-carpeted bare floor living room a pre-transistor Regentone radiogram oscillated in and out of a medium wave pre-pirates BBC radio station.

Tommy Steele had been singing the blues for a few years, and then went all comedy on us and told us the story of the little white bull. At about the same time Lonnie Donegan progressed on the same path from singing hang down your head Tom Dooley about a man about to go to the gallows in the morning to asking us, "Does your chewing gum lose its flavour on the bedpost overnight?"

In playgrounds all over England kids enjoyed the kudos of knowing all the words to both of these essentially naff, tongue in cheek, ditties.

Cliff Richard maintained his respectability when he sang about something called a Livin' Doll long before inflatable women became available. But to be honest we were all still in a dinosaurial age where the song and the singer were king and queen and any instruments employed were poor subjects confined to being just back up devices. A change was in the air.

In the next year the Shadows would twang out Apache, and a one-time session musician called Bert Weedon would come to prominence. Then every kid in the land would want a new fangled electric guitar, buy Bert's instruction book, "Play in Day", and watch his television series of the same name.

My friend John Weeks had a Fender Stratocaster electric guitar and a small amplifier for his birthday. I wanted one, but Mum told me that John had a rich American father who worked for Fords. My dad lived somewhere in deepest Romford 5 miles away with a ginger-haired woman called Renee and worked at the chemical factory in Rainham. He only appeared at Christmas, some birthdays and once a year to take us to Bertram Mill's Circus at Olympia. I never figured out that if John's family were so rich then why did they live in a council house just like ours. Mum was very good at confusing me with convincing arguments.

We weren't exactly a very musical family. The piano in the hall remained unloved and was sold soon after my dad moved out. My German grandfather Maximilian played the violin, my half sister Jutta played the recorder, and my Uncle Friedrich played the accordion. At my oldest half sister Brigitte's wedding Uncle Fredy provided the music. He was that clever that he was able to play by ear. It was literally you hum it son and I'll play it or whatever the equivalent is in German. Heil Hitler! Impressive!

Not many years later the Beatles and the Stones battled for supremacy over the airwaves emanating from the miniaturised transistor radios arriving from Hong Kong, and Radio Caroline broadcast non-stop pop off the Essex coast replacing the annoying BBC, and swapping any allegiance that all teenagers had to Radio Luxembourg. Still in medium wave, Radio Lux 208 had 2 annoying habits. Transmission faded out and was replaced by something Hawkwind used much later in their album In Search of Space. The square-wave-generator-like interference that interrupted the pop tune eventually gave way again to the 208 broadcast usually just as the song was ending. But hold on, none of the songs ever got to the end, because the Luxembourg boys were only allowed to play the first minute of every tune to circumvent a broadcasting regulation of some kind. And that was the other annoyance.

My first serious girlfriend Denise Frost was a petite and sophisticated, well groomed 14 years old. She had twin brothers called Michael and Robert, and their mum bought an acoustic guitar and an electric keyboard for their birthday. I was entrusted to look after these 2 instruments for a couple of weeks before the birthday party and dabbled with the guitar, hurting my fingers, making an awful racket, and getting nowhere.

At the birthday party I met an unkempt kindred spirit called Barry Childs and we quickly became friends. Over the next few years we discovered lots of musical things together, like Bob Dylan, Leonard Cohen, Deep Purple, Hawkwind, Led Zeppelin, Roy Harper, and Pink Floyd, to name but a few. Music and concerts and pubs galore were the order of the day. I was deafened by Deep Purple playing songs from their Deep Purple in Rock album at the Romford Odeon, mesmerised by the virtuosity of Roy Harper at the

Cambridge Folk Festival, disappointed with a lacklustre performance by Bob Dylan at the Isle of Wight Festival, and hypnotised by the intimacy of watching all the best folkies in the Universe playing a few feet away from me in the cellar at Les Cousins Folk Club in Greek Street, Soho. Privilege indeed it was to marvel at the playing and singing of Ralph McTell, Sweeney's Men, Pentangle, including the brilliant Bert Jansch, Tom Paxton, and my favourite Roy Harper. Saturday night and Sunday were set in concrete as Les Cousins all night, a few hours sleep on the Circle Line just after 6 in the morning, followed by brunch, and a protest march usually trailing from Trafalgar Square to the American Embassy in Grosvenor Square in the afternoon. Yes! I was a weekend hippie along with thousands of others. Always returning home on Sunday evening absolutely knackered, and ready to sleep off the weekend before starting up the week again as a respectable suited and booted office waller.

The best thing about Barry apart from the common interest in music was that he had an acoustic guitar, and he knew at least 5 chords. He taught me a little; my fingers hurt, then they bled. I bought books about playing the guitar containing songs that I wanted to learn, and time and again found myself being presented with musical theory on page 5. Bert's "Play in a day" reappeared in my life, and was abandoned very quickly together with at least ten other publications because I wanted to play guitar not learn how to read music. Barry and I both bought nylon string cheapo acoustics to make it easy on our sore left hand fingers. Barry learned a bit of classical, something called Sevillanas, and I strummed my way through the easy 2 chord version of Bob Dylan's song Ramona. The flat, lifeless tone of a nylon string guitar when used for strumming just wasn't good enough for me. So, one Saturday morning when we set off for the Rose-Morris music shop in Shaftesbury Avenue close to Tottenham Court Road tube station, I had my eye on something much better. The Rose-Morris staff were trusting enough to allow anyone to pick up any instrument and have a dabble, and I dared to pick up something rather special. That is where I set my heart on buying my EKO 12-string acoustic guitar, and a week later I'd scrounged the 33 guineas I needed to buy it. It was February 1968, and at last I was equipped to play a proper guitar with excellent tone.

The 12-string was a different sound, a fuller, more exciting experience, and instead of single grooves in my left hand fingers I now developed something akin to railways tracks. Now I had the sound I wanted, the songs came quicker - Blowing in the Wind, Catch the Wind, Desolation Row, She Belongs to Me, and a passable version of Streets of London.

Streets of London was the passport to impressing the girls; the necessary apprenticeship to being recognised as a folkie; the essential repertoire piece of the time, and that was long before it received national acclaim as a Christmas hit in 1974.

Soon, I began to write my own songs, many of which have since vanished into the dustbin of my history. But I also kept lots of lyrics and poems some of which would see the light of day again years later.

What I consider to be my first "worth keeping" song was written in 1973 about my girlfriend at the time. She was a lovely, gentle, dark haired damsel called Annis Harrison, and the song was called "Song to Annis".

The Woodpecker in Hutton Drive was the place to be on any pub night, but especially at weekends. It's now sadly demised as a Tesco Extra, but back in the early 70's I met many a friend there, and most of them played either the guitar, or bass, or keyboards, or drums. There were many very enjoyable jam sessions mostly in very annoyed parent's houses, and that was where I mostly learned that jamming with other friends was one the best ways to learn songs and techniques, and to pick up tricks and clever bits.

So, at long last I'd learned a little of how to play the guitar, my fingers didn't hurt anymore, and could play using either finger-picking or plectrum flat-picking style. Perhaps I wasn't a guitarist because I couldn't do those soaring guitar solos that Clapton, Hendrix, Blackmore and Page seemed to make look so easy. The slurring, sliding, swooning, swooping, orgasmic 10 minute virtuoso performance in the middle of a rock anthem didn't fit easily with acoustic 12-strings. I had a try on friend's electrics including Fender Stratocasters and Gibson Les Pauls, but never quite developed the knack. Amongst all the enigmatic guitar heroes one man stood out, and that was John Aldridge. You've never heard of him, but he was by miles the world's foremost guitar player. He lived with his mum and dad in a tiny council flat less than 100 yards from the Woodpecker, wore scruffy clothes, was habitually out of work, had dubious personal hygiene, and chained smoked Old Holborn roll-ups. But he was the best guitarist who ever walked this Earth.

Then life got in the way. Relationships, marriage to Rosemary, offspring, work, career, mortgages, and making ends meet all interrupted my development and my best friend became an occasional dalliance with the strings. Most times it just gathered dust in the corner, un-played and unloved just like the old piano. But I still put pen to paper, and wrote poems which would one day become songs. Throughout this doldrums period, friends moved on and disappeared from my life, and another friend called Jimmy took up playing electric guitar and joined a band. Fair play to him that he managed to do what I never achieved and learned to play not only electric, but also lead guitar. No! He can't do those soaring solos that I once craved, but he can play a few licks and single note volleys adequately well. Is he a guitarist? No! I don't think he is, because he learns using something called tablature, which is a bit like painting by numbers. So he is a guitar technician whose playing unfortunately lacks true soul and passion, and he has not one single creative bone is his whole body.

Some twenty years later, when bad health eventually befell me with heart attacks and recurring kidney problems, and I managed to pull my local government pension at the age of 48, I suddenly had loads of time on my hands, and the guitar quickly came back into my life. My technique improved, and I started to assimilate different styles into my playing again. Then I began to learn more about complicated stuff like pentatonic scales and blues scales. That is when all the poems and lyrics I had stored up were eventually given life as I turned them into songs.

By then all my favourite guitar virtuosos were old hat, folk music was on its knees, and just like my old friend Jimmy, the music scene had become soulless and lacking in true passion. There were a few exceptions, but mostly the direction had been determined by music factories like Stock, Aitken and Watermann, and then the non-musical gurus like Simon Cowell and Louie Walsh.

In 1998 I was introduced by my double-glazing fitter to one of my neighbours. That is when a lady called Judy came into my life and started to instil in me some confidence of my ability to sing and play.

Judy played guitar and sang her own songs, and so did I, so we were kindred spirits for a while.

In !999, after being seriously ill with kidney failure, and being the closest I'd been to meeting my maker, I began to attend the Church of the Holy Spirit, and it wasn't long before the vicar, Nick Hey, found out that I could play the guitar. I'd been there about 6 months when Nick said to me, "We've got a problem with the church band. Can you help please?"

"What's the problem?" I asked.

"Well," said Nick, "Our guitarist, Pete and his family are moving to Somerset in 2 months time, and we need someone to replace him."

"I don't know if I'm good enough." I replied.

"Give it a try," said Nick, "And we'll talk about it, in a few weeks time."

I turned up for the practice and jammed along with the band, marvelling at how brilliant Pete was, and when it came to the service on Sunday morning I was so grateful that Pete was a gigantic 6 foot 8 tall and stoutly built because I just hid behind him and mimed most of what the band played. But I grew into the role, and Nick never did discuss it any further, so that by the time Pete left and I couldn't hide anymore, I was pretty comfortable with being the band's guitarist. Thus began an 8 year long on and off association with playing in church bands. There is a difference of course, in that playing in church services is not in itself a performance with applause at the end; it's more of a collective celebration with all the glory going to God.

In 2000 I began playing regularly in public at open mike sessions, and then ran the Evelyn Wood Music Club together with Judy for 8 months. I recorded over 70 of my own songs between 2000 and 2008 on demo albums, and collaborated with a few other friends to record about 30 other songs during the same period.

In 2002 and 2003 I passed my exams in musical theory reaching grade 3, but although I have a good understanding I still can't read music. It didn't matter much, because by then we all knew that Bob Dylan, Keith Richard, Eric Clapton and Uncle Tom Cobbley and all, couldn't read music either.

Between 2003 and 2008 I also played in my own band called Redberryash, and we were regulars at open mike sessions all over Essex.

Then, at the end of a 4 year relationship with a very beautiful and talented lady in 2008 I was well and truly down in the mouth, and needed to find a new direction.

After attending creative writing courses and then subsequent writer's group I enjoyed a revival in my writing of stories, poems and songs, and particularly in my song writing and guitar playing ability. Arthritis in my fingers stopped me playing finger-picking style, but I learned to live with it, and developed my flat picking technique instead.

Now I'm confident enough to play on my own at open mike sessions, and it is my intention here in 2015 to go back to the recording studio and record 24 songs which either myself or friends from the writing groups have provided the lyrics for.

So, am I a guitarist?

The answer is an emphatic no!

I can play the guitar, and I understand what I am doing, and what sounds good. I still can't sight read music, and I don't expect I ever will.

Perhaps I am only an adequate singer, but I think I know how to interpret a song and to put my own slant on it. Some would say that of Bob Dylan. So that's a compliment indeed.

I don't know whether John Weeks ever learned to play the guitar at all, or whether Michael and Robert Frost met a third boy and became Emerson, Lake and Palmer. I've no idea what happened in the lives of my friends Barry Childs and John Aldridge, but it is certain that John never received the recognition he undoubtedly deserved.

No, I'm not a guitarist, but I am a singer/songwriter.

And the band played on
(Written 16th/28th March, 2014)

When Charlie's war was over, and the medals were awarded;
brave boys all heading homeward, in straight lines going forward.
In celebration of victory, or humiliation of defeat,
the incessant drum was echoing, all along the street.

Then Chloe's last show closed down, in the theatre at the end of the pier;
washed away like the sands on the beach, gone, no longer here.
There's just the stench of cigarettes, and sickly lukewarm beer,
and the drum will not be silenced, by the cruel, cold atmosphere.

Each life is just another song,
a rhythm and a melody, some words you sing in harmony,
and even if the tune is wrong;
if you're singing in a different key, still in the end it's clear to see,
whether the ride was short or long,
the band still played on.

When the lovers danced their last waltz, and the party was all done;
all the balloons had been deflated, burst and broken just for fun,
all the battles for true love were lost, only greed and lust had won,
through the triumph and the tragedy, the drumbeat still went on.

When Charlie's heart stopped beating, and so he breathed no more
Chloe cast her eyes straight downwards, staring blankly at the floor.
She cried with pain so deep inside, as she stood behind the door.
Charlie was trapped on the outside now, just another pebble on the shore.

Each life is just another song;
a rhythm and a melody, some words you sing in harmony,
and even if the tune is wrong,
if you're singing in a different key, still in the end it's clear to see,
whether the ride was short or long,
the band still played on.

Then Chloe's world was broken, and she lived inside her head.
Not another word was spoken, there was nothing to be said.
She drifted through a wilderness, till her lifeblood dripped no more.
Charlie welcomed her with open arms, when they met on Heaven's shore.

This band has been playing in time since the dawn of creation.
Your ticket for the show lets you go to one destination.
You take chances, make choices, for distractions and for excursions.
You get kicked in the teeth with detours, delays and diversions.
One day you find your time is up, and there's nowhere else to go.
There's no more succour in your cup, there's nothing more to know.

And when the fateful day arrives, for totting up your score,
maybe you'll be wondering, what was all the struggle for.
But the scenes were written just for you,
and you played them from the heart,
and the band will go on playing now, long after you depart.
And the band played on,
And the band played on,
And the band played on.

The Man who sold the World
(Written 1st/4th February, 2016)

When I was just a wee little lad in short trousers and a blue school cap,
my granddad drew me to his side and said, "Son, look at this big map.
Its a map of the world, a mighty big place from sea to shining sea,
and all these bits that are coloured pink, well, they belong to you and me."
"Together they make up the British Empire." he said,
and he said it with such pride.
"Nobody can take it away from us, son
and God knows there are many who've tried."
"That short arsed prat Napoleon couldn't do it at Trafalgar and Waterloo,
and that Charlie Chaplin look-alike, Adolf Hitler fell flat on his face too."

I looked at the map emblazoned with pink
and the names of the faraway places we'd blessed;
big ones like Canada, Australia and India,
New Zealand and great chunks of Africa, east and west,
and then lots of little islands everywhere,
and bases like Gibraltar and Hong Kong,
proud to be British I became that day, and surely that can't be wrong?

"Never forget this," granddad said, "Britannia rules the waves!
Because of that you can be sure Britons never, ever shall be slaves."
Granddad was a man very set in his ways: a man off few words good and true.
He spouted his views through a blurred smoky haze of permanent Old Holborn fumes.

Well time was soon marching onward and Granddad went
to his tobacco farm in heaven,
and soon all those political bigwigs got together
at Downing Street numbers 10 and 11.

"We've got to join this new club called the Common Market." they said;
"Our Empire's going, going, and soon gone."
The trouble was that big nosed frog called General de Gaule
in '63 and '67 kept on saying "Non!"

I read about this French general,
and how we'd saved his country from the Nazi yoke,
And now the ungrateful garlic munching bastard wouldn't let us in.
This must be some kind of joke!

Anyway, one day the pompous twat went the same way
as all the other nobodies.
So we elected a British twat called Sailor Ted, who set his sails for Europe
and enrolled us in the EEC.

Now Sailor Ted was never sure of himself
what with the Miner's Strike and the 3 day week,
so he organised a referendum about the EEC,
and let the people speak.

While this was all happening I read things written
by a singer called Roy Harper;
a much wiser man than Sailor Ted indeed.
What he said about it all was quite cryptic I suppose
but it made good sense to me.

Here goes!

"There was a man from Muddlebro', whose problems he lay down,
upon another's doorstep, in a distant stranger's town.
But forgetting what he'd come for, and in patronising tones,
he gave them all his clothes and bread, to stop their moans and groans.
'It's not your fault where you were born' – he said all condescending;
'We cannot all be made like me with lots of true blue blending.'
'But never mind, I'll pass the hat around our gracious nation.'
The strangers held their laughter back, remembering their station.
Back home, in the Heads of State, the people's memory woke,
and yet the yapping didn't stop, whoever rose and spoke.
But in the fields potatoes flowered, and gulls came with high tides,
and men came back from cutting wood, and gathering by firesides."

So those were the wise words that Roy
told us all back in Sailor Ted's time,
In a tune that he called Referendum.
There he spun out his politics in rhyme.

Now I've become a granddad myself, and in the meantime
many things have changed.
Our relationships with all our European friends have been rearranged,
again and again and again.
There used to be nine countries in the old EEC,
when we joined up in 1973, but somehow,
there are twentyeight countries in all in it
and we're called the European Union now.

What was once a trade federation,
mutually beneficial to buy and sell our things,
has become the United States of Europe,
with a posh flag of 12 stars on a blue background,
arranged in a harmonious ring.

But now the Brussels bureaucrats make our laws,
and they've changed our weights and measures,
opened our borders for free movement of labour,
while they plunder all our treasures.
Our farms are filled with fallow fields;
we can't grow what we want,
And we're forced to buy our food elsewhere,
and get our drink from a foreign font.

We pay homage to a heathen god;
a massive drain on our financial resources,
and every time they're knockers get in a twist,
we're expected to make sacrifices,
to a German lady called Angela who drinks tea at number ten,
while she tells us all what we must do to be good European men.

But there's a saving grace for all,
the possibility of a timely salvation,
because later this year we'll have another referendum,
to decide the future of our once great nation.

Do we really want to stay in this club?
Would it be a disaster if we slung our hook?
Could we please decide things for ourselves again,
and open a new chapter in our glorious history book?

Perhaps when Davis Bowie sang about a man who sold the world,
he was really pointing to Sailor Ted, smiling with his flag unfurled,
skimming the waves with wind filled sails; the oblivious buffoon.
He got peanuts from the monkeys, but was asking for the moon.

My granddad was right to be proud of our nation,
our empire, and our history,
and why we threw it all away is a mystery to me.
Roy Harper's cryptic views are still ringing true,
maybe truer than ever after forty years and more,
And it makes me wonder why we ever contemplated selling cheap,
these wonderful, hallowed, sacred shores.

I don't think we'd be cutting our losses if we said goodbye to the clan.
It's us who's setting them adrift if we stand man to man.
And it was our talent and ingenuity that put the great into our nation;
so let's give Johnny foreigner a Dear John,
and end their exploitation.

Goodbye to Brussels bureaucrats,
aufwiedersehen to Angela too,
let's say to John Bull and the Union Jack,
"We're coming back home to you!"

Footnotes:

In 1963, De Gaulle vetoed the British application to join the EEC.
He declared, "l'Angleterre, ce n'est plus grand chose."
("England is not much any more").
De Gaulle said "Non" again in 1967.
Edward Heath brought us into
European Economic Community or Common Market
On 1st January 1973.
There was another referendum in 1975.

Dangerous Curves
(Written 5th/10th April, 2012)

I'm driving in my Porsche in the dead of night,
roaring through the countryside, blazing headlights,
pedal to the metal, squealing tyres and burning rubber,
shifting through my gears beyond a hundred miles an hour.
I'm your tail gater and I'm bringing up your rear,
I don't want no motorways, no straight roads, or low gears;
want to feel the G-force, the horsepower, and the swerve,
man I'm just a petrol head on dangerous curves.
Dangerous curves, dangerous curves,
man I'm just a petrol head on dangerous curves.
Running my wheels over dangerous curves,
showing my skills on dangerous curves,
moving in for the kill on dangerous curves,
man I'm just a petrol head on dangerous curves.

Dressed up in my finery for nightlife on the pull;
wallet stuffed with ready cash, attitude full of bull (shit),
not looking for that special someone, no just a one night stand;
no long term commitment babes, no-one ties my hands.
I'm God's gift to women, you know I'm the man;
got the looks, got the dosh, ain't no also-ran,
no computer dating, can't get what I deserve;
looking for a lady with dangerous curves.
Dangerous curves, dangerous curves,
looking for a lady with dangerous curves.
Kissing and caressing those dangerous curves,

counting my blessings for dangerous curves,
ain't doing no confessing on dangerous curves,
looking for a lady with dangerous curves.

I went to see the doctor, I was feeling below par;
drove there at breakneck speed in my turbo charged car.
He fixed monitor wires to my body and my head,
he umm'd and ah'd, and took some notes, and this is what he said.
"I've been looking at your test results, so let's not pretend.
Someone here's been burning the candle at both ends.
You'd better slow down my friend, you been living on your nerves;
there's overwhelming evidence for dangerous curves.
Dangerous curves, dangerous curves,
there's overwhelming evidence for dangerous curves.
Live fast, die young, on dangerous curves,
won't last too long on dangerous curves,
one day you'll die on dangerous curves;
there's overwhelming evidence for dangerous curves.

Luftwaffe Reprise
(Written Tuesday 8th May 2012)

Brunhilda Doenitz had arrived in Scotland in December 1980 by accident, an irony that wasn't lost on her. She had been on her way to the wedding of her sister Lisalotte, to Stanley Noble in Yorkshire, when her plane was diverted from Leeds/Bradford by dense fog, and she landed late and annoyed in Glasgow. Certain that she would miss the wedding, she sent a terse wedding telegram to Lisalotte and Stanley which just read "Have a nice wedding. Staying in Scotland. See you later."

She decided to make good use of her bad fortune, and to visit Eaglesham where one of her many heroes had parachuted from his plane in 1941. She knew the story well of how Rudolph Hess had been stupid enough to fly solo to England, so that he could negotiate with Churchill for peace before Hitler launched Operation Barbarossa against Russia in July 1941. How he was only 400 hundred odd miles off course for Chartwell, and his plane had eventually crash landed near Eaglesham, south of Glasgow. Then he was arrested and became a prisoner of war. At the Nuremburg trials he was sentenced to life imprisonment, and spent the rest of his days languishing in Spandau Prison, Berlin, until his death in 1987. When Fraulein Doenitz landed in Glasgow, she saw a parallel with her hero, and it was too good an opportunity to miss, to be able to visit the town where one of her heroes had met his early and humiliating demise. As a lady of genuine Teutonic stock she was proud of her German roots, paradoxically her strength and her weakness at the same time. Her personal heroes were nearly all Germanic icons, and it would be true to say that all of them had flaws, a fact which she found somehow endearing.

She was immediately enraptured with the rugged beauty of the Scottish terrain, and was amazed at how the lack of light pollution in the countryside, and clear, crisp air, displayed the glory of every star in the Milky Way filling the skies. After 2 weeks touring around, and visiting Glasgow, Loch Lomond, Edinburgh, and Perth she eventually settled in Blairgowrie, and found herself a job as a German/English translator. She quickly grew to love her adopted country, and after spending 32 years in Blairgowrie, she considered herself at least a bit Scottish. Sister Lisalotte had maintained some German traits, including bleached blonde hair, and learning pigeon English at best, but Brunhilda had made concessions to her new Vaterland. She liked to wear tartan, and had adopted a gingerish tint to her natural blonde locks.

If little sister was all mouth and trousers, all front and no substance, lots of red lipstick and little grey matter, then big sister was as different as could be. When they were younger they were recognisably sisters, definitely honed from the same fine blade, and both were amply proportioned big-bosomed, blonde women, but over the years more than subtle differences had been accentuated between the two of them.

While they had been working in the Bierkellers at the Munich Beer Festivals, they could both be described as great bustling clod-hoppers of girls. But it was clear which sister was the fairy elephant. Whereas one of the sisters could carry 8 huge steins of beer without spilling a drop, the other had, despite her size, a gazelle-like lightness, a daintiness about her, and only managed 6 at best. She was ambi-dextrous, and could write equally well with both hands. Her sister was single-minded, but could get muddled equally well with both halves of her brain.

The older sister by just under 2 years WAS fur coat and no knickers, red hat no drawers, strong of arm but certainly not thick of head. She was a positive, extrovert and intelligent woman. To her, political correctness was utter nonsense, and she called it as it really was. She took no prisoners, and would have been a perfect foil for Hugh Ramsbottom.

The little town of Blairgowrie, nestling at the foot of the Grampian Mountains had grown in the intervening years, so much so that by 2012 it was the "twin burgh" of Blairgowrie and Rattray. It was the raspberry growing centre of the Universe, and himbeere as they were known in Germany were the exiled German lady's favourite fruit. Blairgowrie was also only a short distance from the village of Bankfoot, the location of the Macbeth Experience, where she worked part time every summer season. She adored the intrigue and mystery surrounding Macbeth. The question as to whether he was the murderer portrayed in the "Scottish Play" by William Shakespeare, or an 11th century Scottish warrior king fascinated her. She was a romantic soul, and also loved the connections with and proximity to Glamis Castle, which was not only the setting for Shakespeare's Macbeth, but also the childhood home of Elisabeth Bowes-Lyon, the Queen Mother. Despite the overtly republican credentials of her many heroes, she was resolute in her admiration for the British Royal Family. She thought, "Weren't they really all German anyway?"

On the evening of her birthday on May 8th she had been at a local protest meeting, to campaign against plans to erect a wind turbine on the top of Balduff Hill, so close to the local beauty spot of Reekie Linn, a beautiful and impressive waterfall in Genisla. She had two very strong personal reasons for resisting this planned project.

First of all, Balduff Hill was a favourite launch site for her hang gliding exploits, one of her various aeronautical pursuits. Secondly, the Reekie Linn waterfall held great sentimental significance for her. A long time ago, shortly after her accidental adoption of Scotland as her new home, she had fallen in love with a young man called Henry McVitie, and they had often made their way up to the waterfall in the twilight of the long Scottish July evenings, They were "roaming in the gloaming" as the well known song would have said. And it was there that she was certain she had conceived her only son Duncan, lying on a dark green and blue Mack tartan blanket listening to the incessant, powerful, overwhelming rush of the waterfall in heavy spate, as a balmy evening lingered on into seductive, quieter semi-darkness. She didn't have any "green" disagreements with wind turbine construction. She thought they were an excellent idea. It was just a case of NIMBY- "not in my back yard" and she was determined to stop the erection of a wind turbine on HER hill next to HER waterfall.

During her time in Germany she had been an ardent fan of an electronic music band called Tangerine Dream, and particularly their famed work Phaedra released in 1974. When she became an accidental Brit, with an uncharacteristic capriciousness she switched her allegiance to Hawkwind, a space rock group, and as they had gone "In Search of Space" in 1971, so she went in search of Hawkwind in 1980. She found them in concert at the Perth Theatre, and it was there that she met the brawny, handsome 20 year old Henry McVitie, who at that time had the nickname "Biscuits" for rather obvious reasons. It was this Scottish patriot who would become her son Duncan's father

A few years before he had become disillusioned with his job as a builder's labourer, and having learned to play blues guitar, and equipped with an abundance of youthful audacity, he had engineered bumping into Dave Brock the leader of Hawkwind, with the idea of persuading him to let him join the band. The space cowboys were nothing like a blues band, but Dave was amused by the boy's bravado, and offered him a job as a roadie. When Brunhilda cheekily sneaked backstage and into the green room at the Perth Theatre, Henry was three sheets to the wind, and so wearing his beer goggles he mistook her for the legendary Stacia. She was a big Irish girl who had been a regular attraction at early 70's Hawkwind concerts, dancing nude and often adorned by iridescent paint. He was ribbed by the band members for uttering the classic, "Hello Babe, I didn't recognise you with your clothes on!"

She didn't mind his drunkenness, she'd seen plenty of drunken men in the Bierkellers, and he was her kind of man. He wore a kilt, rode a motorcycle, and was a ginger-haired, long-bearded Scottish patriot. Soon they were inseparable, and she followed him all over Scotland and the North of England as the band continued their tour. But she knew he was tied to his touring life with the band, a nomad who wouldn't be shackled, and so when she found she was carrying his child, there was no way she was going to tie him down.

Her only beloved son wasn't the sordid product of a one night stand however, because through the years groupie and roadie had frequently met up again, and rekindled their fire, whenever Hawkwind, and later also Motorhead were on tour. He became the love of her life, and she was willing to make this sacrifice for him. Although when they met, he bore the nickname of "Biscuits", throughout most their long intermittent relationship she knew him by the name of "Tusker".

This came about when Henry worked as a roadie for Lemmy and Motorhead. He lost the epithet "Biscuits" one night when the intimacy, craziness and camaraderie of travelling on the road together with the band led to a drunken willy measuring contest. Bernard, one of the other roadies, who claimed to have the biggest plonker in Scotland, was devastated to find that "Biscuits" was such a big boy, a well endowed, indeed, donkey-blessed individual. He immediately renamed the boy because of his elephantine proportions, and he adopted his new name with pride, and so became known by all as "Tusker".

The day after Brunhilda's 60th birthday, a Tuesday, was a fresh and breezy May morning, and she awoke happy and content. After a breakfast of pumpernickel black rye bread with marmalade, and strong coffee, she said "Aufwiedersehen" to her son as he made his way off to work in Perth. She was proud of her son, who had qualified as an accountant 7years ago, and was now working at a company called Perth Open Office Services. P.O.O.S. were a major company, with contracts all over Scotland for the generation and installation of office premises, covering everything from office furniture and computers, to paperclips, and coffee machines. As he left his mother with a routine nonchalance, to enjoy her daily interests, neither of them knew how significant this day would be in their lives, and how their lives would change forever.

After Duncan had left for work, she went down to her den in the cellar, in her small, tidy bungalow on the outskirts of town. It was a place that was habitually out of bounds to her son, her secret place, where she was able to indulge in another one of her passions. She emerged from the cellar an hour later, and loaded up the trailer of her Freelander with her hang-glider. The springtime sun had warmed the heather-clad hills of Angus, sucked up the early morning dew, and it looked like the perfect day for flying had arrived.

Soon she was on her way, fully equipped for another beautiful solo flight. She had many passions, but flying was her most satisfying, and most rewarding. It was flying with a difference, because she combined it with her passion for naturism. She was a founder member of the Blairgowrie and District Naturist Aeronautics Club. The BADNACers - as they were known, supported many flying disciplines, and these included hang-gliding, micro-lighting, free-fall parachuting, and gliding, all of them nude, and with their own unique risk elements. It was clear that with all of these pursuits, the flyer had to be very, very careful especially when landing. Landing in the wrong place was risky anyway, but even more so when naked.

Brunhilda had always been fascinated by the prospect of being able to soar through the skies, but just ordinary flying on a scheduled airline flight was far too tame, and removed all that was best from the experience. To her it wasn't real flying, it was a boring undertaking. She just considered it as cocooned in a sterile cylinder together with a hypnotised collection of ignorant morons, whose only purpose in being there was the destination, and to whom the flying experience was mostly a claustrophobic time-consuming nuisance. She just thought "Where was the freedom, the excitement, the wind rushing through your nostrils, and across your bare skin, and the over all feeling of being in control of the elements, and ultimately your own fate?"

Her first introduction to the thrills of real flying came when she had met her kindred spirit, the love of her life. She and "Tusker" had discovered that they had a common interest in flying, and it happened that he regularly went gliding from Portmoak Airfield at Scotlandwell, and was a founder member of Flying Unhindered Club Kinross. She remembered the absolute thrill of that first flight over the Ochil Hill ridges and high over Loch Leven, and the Lomond Hills. On an outstanding clear day with superb visibility, she was ecstatic to see across both the rivers Forth and Tay and as far afield as the Grampian Mountains, all the time mesmerised by the almost silent swooping and soaring of the glider. She was nothing short of knocked-out, hooked, and from that point on flying in all its free forms became a lifelong obsession. Not much later when she had learned to fly solo, she added the naturist element, and that came about because she believed that another one of her heroes had been very fond of flying nude.

Hermann Goering might have been best known as a swaggering, fat, arrogant, Nazi bullyboy, the Luftwaffe chief, who stole art treasures from all over Europe in World War 2 for his personal art collection, and when indicted for war crimes at Nuremburg escaped justice when he managed to commit suicide the day before he was scheduled to be executed. But Fraulein Doenitz preferred to remember him as a veteran of World War I, as an ace fighter pilot with 22 victories, and a recipient of the coveted Blue Max. He was also the last commander of the "Flying Circus", Jagdgeschwader 1; the fighter wing once led by Manfred von Richthofen, "The Red Baron", another of her heroes. In line with her adulation for failed heroes, she also liked Hermann's sense of humour. She was amused that apparently he once wired Hitler after his visit to the Vatican "Mission accomplished. Pope unfrocked. Tiara and pontifical vestments are a perfect fit." She was unamused that when he had degenerated from the once-dashing and muscular fighter pilot, into a corpulent, even obese, figure of fun, Germans joked about his ego, saying that "He would wear an Admiral's uniform to take a bath.", and joking that "He sits down on his stomach."

Soon after getting her solo gliding credentials, Brunhilda enjoyed the thrill of parachuting from the Perth (Scone) Airfield, and shortly after that from a Dundee airfield near the Tay Bridge. She then became a pioneer of the practice of nude free fall parachuting. Personally she found no difficulty in this, but in training others to enjoy this experience, she quickly discovered there was a requirement for some sort of qualification, and certification. This came about after a series of nude parachuting "accidents" which occurred when participants who had become very excited during the freefall, suddenly relaxed as soon as the parachute opened. The result was a high incidence of what was known as high altitude muck-spreading at 3,000 feet.

She drove confidently, as she had so many times before, from her bungalow in Dunkeld Road through the Blairgowrie town centre, and out along the A926 towards Aylth, then left along the B954 up to Bridge of Craigisla next to Reekie Linn. She then opened a gate onto the farmland that took her off-road up towards the summit of Balduff Hill at 1394 feet above sea level. In brilliant sunshine she carefully assembled her hang-glider, which she had painted red in homage to another of her heroes, and sported a brilliant red sail, and then donned her specially adapted crash helmet. This had been modified to include an MP3 player, which played her favourite gliding tune on a continuous short loop. She never took to the skies without this little extra. Her music of choice was a song she had first heard as a young girl of 14, back in 1966. It was the Royal Guardsmen singing Snoopy versus the Red Baron. Whilst hanging in the warm air, searching out a friendly rising thermal she would sing at the top of her voice.

> "After the turn of the century,
> In the clear blue skies over Germany,
> Came a roar and a thunder men had never heard,
> Like the screamin' sound of a big war bird.
> Up in the sky, a man in a plane,
> Baron von Richthofen was his name,
> Eighty men tried and eighty men died,
> Now they're buried together on the country side."

She loved the song, almost as much as she loved her ultimate flawed hero.

Manfred Albrecht Freiherr von Richthofen was widely known as the Red Baron, owing to the fact that he had his aircraft painted red. He was another World War I ace fighter pilot, another recipient of the Blue Max, and considered the top ace of that war, being officially credited with 80 victories. She delighted in Richthofen's many other nicknames including "Le Diable Rouge" ("Red Devil") or "Le petit Rouge" ("Little Red") in French, and the "Red Knight" in English.

Fully kitted up, she stripped off stark naked, and placed her clothes in a rucksack, which she strapped tightly on her back. She picked up the hang-glider, and with all the bravado born of many years experience, and despite her 60 years, she dashed headlong towards the edge, taking off into the wildest, bluest yonder singing away at the top of her voice. It was an excellent flying day, and the thermals were kind. She had wonderful views over Cairn Gibbs and Loch of Lintrathen, and then she circled back towards Alyth, and on in a wide arc back towards Balduff Hill still singing away. Many times she chuckled her contented flying ace way through the song's chorus:-

> "Ten, twenty, thirty, forty, fifty and more,
> The bloody Red Baron was rollin' up the score,
> Eighty men died tryin' to end that spree,
> Of the bloody Red Baron of Germany."

Replete with her success, she decided not to land, but to fly on, and complete the circuit again. The views at first were better than ever. She flew on, and sang on:-

> "In the nick of time, a hero arose,
> A funny lookin' dog, with a big black nose.
> He flew into the sky to seek revenge,
> But the Baron shot him down; "Curses! Foiled again!"
> Ten, twenty, thirty, forty, fifty and more,
> The bloody Red Baron was rollin' up the score,
> Eighty men died tryin' to end that spree,
> Of the bloody Red Baron of Germany."

As she tried to make the turn back towards Balduff Hill for the second time, there was an abrupt change in the weather. The sunshine had suddenly gone, and she found herself shivering in the first spray of a light rain. Struggling to control the hang-glider she resolved to land as quickly as possible. The continuous loop of her favourite flying song still played, but she had stopped singing as she struggled for control.

> "Now Snoopy'd swore that he'd get that man,
> So he asked the great pumpkin for a new battle plan.
> He challenged the German to a real dog fight,
> While the Baron was laughing, he got him in his sight.
> The bloody Red Baron was in a fix;
> He tried everything, but he'd run out of tricks.
> Snoopy fired once, then he fired twice,
> And the bloody Red Baron was spinnin' out of sight."

The MP3 player never got to the chorus, before she found herself swirling continuously round in a freak tornado. In a very short while, totally out of control, she came down in a huge thistle patch close to the Devil's Elbow, on the 17th fairway of the Blairgowrie Lansdowne Golf Course. And here she died the death of a thousand needles as she was prickled to death being dragged round and round, in and out of the thistles for more than 10 minutes. Up in heaven she would probably have seen the irony of dying on the wing au naturel, whilst listening to a song about her beloved ace fighter pilot.

Brunhilda's G. P. Doctor McPherson just happened to be playing the golf course at the time, and he was sheltering in the trees at the edge of the fairway when the tornado swirled its way towards the thistles. He and his golfing colleagues had seen the hang-glider crash, and had witnessed the prickly demise. She was pronounced dead at the scene, and her remains were removed to a local undertaker immediately. Details for contacting her son Duncan were found in her rucksack, and he was informed of the accident at about 1 pm.

Duncan made his way back to Blairgowrie as quickly as he could, visited his mother at the undertakers, cried quietly, and then went home shocked and devastated. He might have been 30 years old, but he was a "mummy's boy" in the sense that there had only been one significant woman in his life. He had never had a girlfriend, but he wasn't stifled by his mother, and otherwise he was no habitual social misfit. A complex character, a Scot with German undertones, unperturbed by being the illegitimate son of Henry a father he never knew, he accepted these building blocks, and they never really bothered him too much.

His first thoughts back at the bungalow were how casually he had left home that morning, going through the daily routines, and unaware of how his life would change that day. The undertakers had returned the rucksack, and when he went through the contents he found instructions on how to carry on with his life. His mother, organised and methodical to the last, was always aware of the risks she encountered with her flying pursuits, and she had prepared everything for the possibility of her demise while flying. Amongst her effects was an envelope for her son. It was addressed:

"To my lovely boy, Duncan. To be opened after I have flown to Heaven. xxx"

He sat down, his hands were shaking, and tears rolled down his cheeks as he fumbled with the envelope. Inside was a single sheet of paper, and a large brass key. The letter, in Brunhilda's handwriting read:-

"My dearest wee boy Duncan,
I am so sorry that I can't be with you any longer.
You are a fine, handsome boy, and I have always done my best for you. I have   guarded many secrets from you for a long time. But I promised myself that one day, after my death the truth would be revealed. I want you to find someone for me, and make sure he is at my funeral. His name was Henry "Tusker" McVitie, and he was the only man I ever loved. He'll be in his 50's now. I have no address for him, but if you get in touch with Lemmy from Motorhead saying you are Brunhilda from Blairgowrie, then I am sure Tusker can be found. In this envelope is the key to my cellar, a secret place for me. What you will find in there will make you a very rich man.
Goodbye my precious lovely boy.
Love Mum xxx"

Westward Ho! Ho! Ho!
(Written as a script for a short play, 19th October, 2014)
(Rewritten as a story 30th December 2014 to 6th January 2015)

One evening in the spring of 1492 Queen Isabella and King Ferdinand, (Isabel y Fernando, los Reyes Católicos) were holding court in the Alcazar in Cordoba on the banks of the Guadalquivir River. Present with the King and Queen were a few trusted confidantes, Carlos Domingo Rodriguez, Ricardo Francisco Garcia, and the King's favourite confidante Pedro Velasquez del Lago de Valladolid.

The King was sitting in a very grand chair. He groaned, "I hate conducting official business in the evening. Do we have to do this now?"

The Queen was sitting in an even more ostentatious throne. She sighed.

"What do you mean? After you've drunk 2 bottles of our very best Rioja and eaten yourself immovable again?"

"Don't be like that, Queenie. You know I like to be entertained with a bit of flamenco dancing on these rainy evenings."

"Yeah! You've always been a sucker for swirly skirts and maximum derriere, my dear. But we do have royal matters to attend to."

The King stood up, and put his hands on his hips, "Yes, But it's that fucking Ligurian navigator, Cristobal Colon who calls himself Christopher Columbus, the Wop from Genoa again. I thought we dismissed his ludicrous plans to find a route to the Spice Islands by sailing West back about 6 years ago."

The favourite confidante, Velasquez was used to these little bickering sessions between the royals. He knew that both of them had strong views, and liked to get their own way. Queen Isabella 1 had ruled Castile, and King Ferdinand ll was the monarch of Aragon before they had married and united their different kingdoms in October 1469. It had always irked Ferdinand that Isabella was a year older than him. Velasquez spoke slowly, and in a considered and careful statement he uttered, "If I may concur with your majesty. You are quite correct. Columbus sought an audience with the court after your majesties glorious marriage had united the many kingdoms of the Iberian Peninsula. On 1 May 1486 Columbus presented his plans to our Queen Isabella, who, in turn, referred them to a committee."

"That's correct," said the Queen, "That was after he had already been to see that disfigured upstart, our sworn enemy, King John II, of Portugal in 1485, and been given the bum's rush because the Genoan dickhead totally underestimated the travelling distance to the Spice Islands."

Velasquez spoke again, addressing himself only to the King who had returned to his chair, "I remember that Columbus proposed that your majesty equip three sturdy ships and grant him one year's time to sail out into the Atlantic, search for a western route to the Orient, and return."

The King laughed and the Queen scoffed, and all three confidantes politely echoed their mirth. The Queen hated Velasquez, and the way he had achieved his lofty position as the King's confidante. In private she referred to him as, "The smelly fisherman", because of his dishevelled, and unkempt appearance, and the fact that he had been a poor pescador in Valladolid before he had the good fortune to rescue the King from a watery grave when he had gone for a swim after drinking too much Rioja.

Rodriguez was the Queen's favourite, and felt the need to say something, "Columbus also requested he be made "Great Admiral of the Ocean", appointed governor of any and all lands he discovered, and given one-tenth of all revenue from those lands."

The Queen laughed," Typical man, asks for far too much, and gets nothing for his trouble."

Ferdinand began swigging from a bottle of Tempranillo Rioja, and then giggling like a child. Then he said, "Didn't put him off though, did it? No, good old Chris Colon, goes back and tries again. Lived up to his funny name didn't he?"

As usual the Queen felt the need to rebuke her younger husband, "Why are you so crude after you've had a drink, my dear? If you think he's an arsehole why don't you just come out and say it?"

The King was used to ignoring her frequent need to chastise him.

Rodriguez wanted to show that he was more knowledgeable than "The smelly fisherman", and continued," If I may bring us back to the matter in hand your majesties. In 1488, Columbus appealed to the court of Portugal once again, and that meeting also proved unsuccessful."

Velasquez not wishing to be outdone quickly added," I believe he drew a blank because soon after that audience, Bartolomeu Dias returned to Portugal with news of a successful rounding of the southern tip of Africa near the Cape of Good Hope."

Rodriguez went on, enjoying the verbal battle," With an Eastern sea route to Asia apparently at hand, King John the Portuguese pervert was no longer interested in Columbus's far-fetched project."

The King was eager to take control of any argument between the two confidantes, and sneered," And ever since then the misguided mariner's been banging on our door trying to persuade us to finance his fantasies. I suppose now that he's living in Cordoba he thinks he can pop round for a Paella Valenciana any time he likes."

"God, I hate paella, can't stand all that seafood with eyes on my plate." said the Queen.

There was a pause in the conversation while the King opened another bottle of wine, and poured a huge glass out for each of the confidantes. Then he raised his glass in the air saying, "Cheers mates."

The men all raised their glasses and swallowed hard.

The Queen looked on scornfully and knew it was a very typical wind up, and uttered derisorily, "Yeah, Bottoms up King Lush, and you'll have one of your headaches in the morning, el cabezota."

Garcia was nobody's favourite, and owed his position in the court to a long time family connection through the Queen's father. He had been very patient, and had so far just watched the points scoring unfold. Having been totally silent so far, he was becoming irritated with the lack of focus in the discussion. Now it was his chance to take control and exert his more mature attitude over the royals and their confidantes.

He asked, "So, are your majesties going to see Columbus this evening, or shall I send him on his way?"

The King thought for a while, as he was inclined to do whenever Garcia contributed to their debates, and everybody else waited for the wheels to turn. Despite having drunk more than his fill, he suddenly waxed very lucid, saying, "So, we've rejected Chris the arsehole before on the advice of our confessors and savants because he grossly underestimated the distance to Asia going westward. Now there is a route East around Africa it all seems a bit pointless."

Velasquez took up the gauntlet by replying," May I remind your majesty that in order to keep Columbus from taking his ideas elsewhere, and to keep our options open, you gave him an annual allowance of 12,000 maravedis and, in 1489, furnished him with a letter ordering all cities and towns under our domain to provide him with food and lodging at no cost."

Queen Isabella laughed, "That was probably another great night for our wine suppliers, my dear."

King Ferdinand ignored her jibe and continued, "OK, so let's think about it. The little Wop thinks the World is round, and he can get to Asia sailing westward. So, what are the possibilities?"

Velasquez was quickest, "He's wrong, the World is flat and he falls off the edge and is never seen again."

Rodriguez added his first thought, "He get's shipwrecked in a storm, and is stranded on a desert island."

Velasquez grinned at the thought, adding, "And is never seen again."

Garcia wanted to get back into the conversation, and all he could offer was, "The 3 ships he wants are attacked and he is eaten by sea dragons."

Velasquez repeated, "And is never seen again."

The King enjoyed setting the advisors against each other, and paused while he put his hand up to his mouth, and then took another slug of wine, before saying, "Or, and it is possible, he finds what he's looking for and comes back with lots of spices and other stuff."

Queen Isabella changed her tune and immediately revived her interest, adding, "And with shiploads of gold and silver."

"Could it be?" quizzed Ferdinand.

Quickly his royal wife continued her train of thought with, "And maybe some decent exotic new food to eat, so I don't have to suffer any more bloody paella."

As all the men laughed, the King mischievously seemed to change his mind and the direction of the debate with, "We could just abandon the whole idea and hand the smarmy git over to Uncle Tom."

Velasquez was familiar with his boss's frequent changes in train of thought, and anticipating that neither of the other two advisors would be quick enough to respond, he said to his King, "Your majesty, the Grand Inquisitor, Tomás de Torquemada, has done a magnificent job cleaning up our glorious nation, and his triumphant work since 1478 in spreading the Spanish Inquisition from Castile throughout the lands is well recognised. We sanctioned his establishment of tribunals in Sevilla, Jaén, Córdoba, Ciudad Real and Saragossa. We could send a messenger to get him here right now."

Rodriguez, however was on to the new direction with unnerving rapidity, and said to his Queen," Your majesty may find that Tomas is very busy at the moment extraditing Jews from our realm. He has a big project under way after the edict of March 31st, the Alhambra Decree."

Garcia decided to trump both of his rivals by saying, "Ah, but his vicious sidekick Cardinal Francisco Jiménez de Cisneros would relish the job of getting rid of Columbus, he hates all foreigners."

The King responded, "Oh Yes, the Red Cardinal. He is a sadistic little bastard. He could do the job, torture old Colon, and then bump him off."

"Oh, my dear God", interjected the Queen, "Before you drunken lot get carried away have you really considered all the options. Think about it. If we give Columbus what he asks for there are only 2 possibilities. He disappears or he comes back. If he disappears; problem solved. If he returns we will have stolen a march on the Portuguese, the French, the Dutch and the English."

The King was off again on another different tack, but only to throw the Queen off track, "I wonder what the Pope thinks. We are all good Catholics, and we mustn't upset him."

"Well, we do know that some popes have regarded the idea of the World being anything but flat as pure heresy, and set about executing anybody with opposing views, even though Aristotle suggested a spherical realm in the 4th century BC." instructed Velasquez.

"But I am pretty sure that the current incumbent at the Vatican, Pope Alexander VI, whom we all know as ambidextrous Alex, is very busy converting little boys to Christianity in his own unique way. You could say he has his attention permanently diverted to small things." added Garcia.

There were dirty laughs all round, except for the Queen, who frowned, and said, "Get back to the point boys. I'm tired, and it'll soon be time for my bath."

"OK, what do think we should do Queenie?" said Ferdinand, grasping a crafty opportunity to end the debate.

"Send Columbus on his way." directed Isabella, and added, "I don't like him, he looks shifty to me, he has webbed feet, and bad breath."

The King's plan was working, "That's settled then." he said, "Pedro, do the honours will you?"

Velasquez bowed and left the room. The Queen went off for her bath.

The King opened a bottle of Moscatel de Valencia.

Later that same evening in the Alcazar in Cordoba there was another meeting of King Ferdinand, his confidante Pedro Velasquez, and Cristóbal Colón.

By this time the King was well sozzled. In a drunken slur he said to his guest, "Sorry about that Chris old son. It was the little woman who sent you away. You know she's a year older than me, and thinks she always knows everything better. So, you want 3 ships, a year's sailing time, and all that other stuff about "Great Admiral of the Ocean", a big share of the spoils etc. etc. Right?"

Columbus realised that the King was drunk, and that he had the upper hand, and replied courteously, "If your majesty so desires and will grant."

In undue haste the King said, "OK, Chris, consider it done. Put it there my son.", and he and Columbus joined in a high five.

Ferdinand raised his glass, and added, "Bien Vacaciones and all that bollocks Chris. Pedro here will sort out the detail for you. Oh, and make sure you bring me back some gold and silver, and some tasty foody items for the missus will you?"

Columbus bowed and left the room, and the King turned to his confidante Velasquez with a contented drunken grin for a job well done trumping his little Queenie by taking the decision making away from her and Rodriguez.

"Am I brilliant or what Pedro? "he smarmed, "The best king that ever graced the Spanish throne, any throne for that matter. What I say goes. I am so wise, I should never be challenged. Am I not the wisest, most intelligent man that ever lived? Well, tell me the truth Pedro my old mucker, is that not so?"

Velasquez replied, "Your majesty is surely aware that I always tell him the truth."

"No, don't mess about, come on, we're mates aren't we? Give me the bottom line, Pedro. Do I tell it like it is?"

"With your majesty's permission I would caution you to be circumspect."

"You'll have to run that past me a bit slower, my friend." said the King revelling in his victory while laughing in his stupor.

Velasquez considered his words and then explained, "Your majesty, even the wisest and most revered king must understand that in the protocols of discussion we are all separate beings with our own views and fears and aspirations. We must all, whatever our standing in this world, respect the opinions of others, even if we disagree. It is extremely easy to confuse oneself by assuming that everything we utter is an indisputable fact, and not merely just our personal opinion. Conversely, we can also fall into the trap of automatically assuming that everything anyone else utters is merely an opinion to be dismissed especially if we disagree with them. Respect must always be amicably afforded to the views of others whether or not we are in agreement with them. Life is a vast learning curve, and the wisest of men are perennially open to fresh ideas and viewpoints."

Ferdinand was bemused.

"Hmmm! OK, Pedro. So, is the World flat or round?"

"Well, your majesty, we must keep our minds open to both viewpoints. However wise and mighty, and all knowing we are. You must even as the greatest and most revered king be aware that what you say and do is based on your personal view of the world and the people in it. Your opinions are not facts, and you must not react to disagreement with hostility and aggression. Everybody's opinions are equally valid from the highest king to the lowest peasant."

"You're so right Pedro, what would I do without you, my most trusted confidante?"

The royal court was in session again at the Alcazar in Cordoba on 20th March 1493. Present were the King and Queen, and trusted confidantes, Rodriguez, Garcia, Velasquez, and Christopher Columbus recently returned from his voyage.

The King was sober for a change, and greeted the adventurer, "How's it going Chris? Got any gold, silver or exotic food?"

Columbus was very pleased with himself and replied, "Yes indeed your majesty. We have acquired much treasure for our kind benefactor's greater glory, and many strange new foods."

The Queen shifted excitedly on her throne, "Bloody marvellous! What have you got to eat then?" she asked.

Columbus was confident of his host's approval saying, "Your majesty's treasurer is weighing the gold and silver as we speak, and here are our food items from the New World."

He began to open several large sacks, and wanted to wallow in the delight for each item he had discovered before handing them to the others. But the King interrupted him, "So you didn't find a way to the Spice Islands by going west then?"

Columbus replied smiling, "No, but we found new lands that will bring your royal highnesses much wealth and prominence. I named our first landfall San Salvador."

The Queen was becoming impatient and insisted, "What about the food?"

Columbus began describing the items he had returned with.

"These brown blobby things are potatoes. You boil and eat them."

"Yuk!" said Isabella.

"These leaves are called tobacco. You crush and smoke them."

"Right on!" said Ferdinand.

"These red pointy things are chillies. They will add fire to your food."

"Now you're talking." said the Queen.

"These red round things are tomatoes; a sweet fruit."

"Oh Yes!" said the Queen.

"This funny looking, noisy bird clucking round my feet is a chicken, a very nice tender white meat."

"Don't like the clucking, looking forward to eating you birdie." said the Queen.

"And these small brown pods are crushed to make a delightful confectionary called chocolate."

"Wow!" gushed the Queen.

"Blimey! Well done Chris." said the King, "I suppose that you'll want us to finance some more trips then?"

Columbus adopted his most pleading countenance, "If your majesty would be so kind." he whined condescendingly.

The Queen still didn't like the web-footed, bad-breathed sailor, and just wanted to see and sample the plunder. She wanted to dismiss him quickly, and so she asked, "Can you sum it all up then quickly Christopher, 'cause we're a bit busy thinking about raising an armada to conquer the English right now."

Columbus seized the moment to consolidate his plea for further expeditions, and explained succinctly, "OK. This is the bottom line. We had 3 ships, La

Santa María, La Niña, and La Pinta. We set off not knowing where we were going. We arrived not knowing where we were. And we returned not knowing where we had been. But all in all it was a highly successful expedition. Perhaps our voyage was based on supposition, ignorance, if not a lack of knowledge, and possibly sheer luck, but it still had enormous validity and significance. Best of all we return with great treasures for your majesties."

"Yeah! Too right! Thanks Chris." said the King, "Fancy a glass or 6 of Rioja to celebrate?"

Perhaps at least one of the Spanish royals had secretly hoped that Columbus would be lost at sea and never return. Whilst they were both delighted with the gold and silver, it was clear they were confused over the food items he had brought back. Later that night they smoked some potato and chilly cigarettes, and dined on boiled tobacco with chicken cooked in chocolate, followed by a dessert of tomatoes in custard.

Oh Happy Day?
(Written 21st October 2016)

The Wakahisa family had woken early to another lovely bright sunny August day, but now away from the noisy buzz of the city, and peacefully at ease in the forest clearing that was home to Uncle Yori and Auntie Hanako. I watched, happily invisible, in the lower branches of a tall red cedar, as the children played happily. The three boys ran around in the nearby trees, hiding, jumping out to surprise each other, careering around like a mad posse, shouting and jeering, full of big smiles and laughter. Little Yoko sat quiet on a swing in the garden with Michiko on her lap singing softly to herself. It was her 8th birthday. Nariko was busy gathering wild flowers from a sunny slope at the back of Uncle Yori's log cabin. Takuma and Nosomi had been for a short stroll in the forest, holding hands and smiling at each other. The couple who lived on Mount Ohmine were employed in their daily chores; Yori was chopping firewood and Hanako was preparing some food for breakfast. The warm blue skies above them were filled with late summer promise. The clearing was surrounded by a diverse collection of mature oak, maple, chestnut and beech trees, standing proudly, honouring the Earth beneath and the Heavens above.

This was a small paradise in a turbulent war torn world.

Suddenly, time stood still; the leaves ceased to rustle on the welcome breeze that drifted lazily from the greenness of the tall trees surrounding the homestead. The forest held its breath as flocks of birds took flight in panic and flew swiftly out of the trees and headed westward, and there was a dead stifling silence. In seconds Takuma had gathered his family around him as they watched, and trembled in utter disbelief at something strange and fearsome happening in the distance, over the city that they had walked away from the previous day. The most brilliant and intense white light, like a thousand suns shining all at once, filled the skies obliterating the perfect blue horizon. They all shielded their eyes and cowered down towards the sanctuary of the ground. Uncle Yori beckoned the whole family towards him, and as quick as gazelles being chased by a lion they followed him through a narrow ditch that led to a small cave underneath the log cabin. Then a loud boom like a mountain crashing on to the Earth filled their ears, and made Mount Ohmine tremble and shake like the most terrifying earthquake. It seemed that every molecule of the atmosphere was being sucked together and shrunk and then being hurtled violently outwards again in a reverberating wave, and this was happening a million times in a split second. Then the whole forest swayed westwards in a gigantic arboreal tidal wave accompanied by the sound of air rushing across the mountain in an eccentric hurricane. Every member of the family lay flat and belly down on the cold rock, hands over their ears, eyes closed, not daring to breathe, dry mouthed and wet eyed, until the noise of a booming that broke the skies, and the rushing that drove the wind, was spent. My ghostly presence waited with them tucked into a crevice in the rock wall. A short time that felt like millennia passed.

Uncle Yori was the first to move. Slowly he crept outside and I floated behind, following him up the incline of the narrow ditch. He still needed to shield his eyes from the light, and the air felt strangely warm in a very uncomfortable way, as if an alien, crushing, choking wind was blowing across the landscape. The rest of the family followed until we were all outside again looking down the mountain in terrified silence. When it became possible to focus out to the distance, an incredible, unbelievable sight confronted all of us. The City of Hiroshima had disappeared from the face of the Earth, and had been replaced by a raging fire burning with all the violence and intensity of an erupting volcano. And above the place where the city had been a massive billowing mushroom cloud was surging its way 10 miles up into the sky.

Takuma began to cry, partly because the home that he had lived in for his whole life had been wiped off the planet, and partly because he finally understood why the voices and whispers had been telling him to leave. Nosomi eyes were filled with tears as she gathered the children around her and quietly explained that they could never go back to their home.

"I don't mind, Mummy," Yoko smiled, "Me and Michiko like it here at Uncle Yori's house."

Then I found myself in another place. Again I was in a plane, a very similar aircraft to "Enola Gay", but all the faces on board were different. I looked around me trying to work out what was going on. One of the crew was busily occupied wielding a large camera apparatus as another man was reading out loud in a deadpan voice while writing on a clipboard.

"Warm day, blue skies,
perfect visibility,
8.15 am Japanese time,
"Little Boy" released,
at 31,000 feet.
District Nakajima-cho,
t-shaped Aioi bridge,
target on the River Ota,
over Hiroshima.
Wait 45 seconds until,
detonation successful,
2,000 feet above ground level.
Intense white light,
very loud explosion,
estimated spread 3 miles wide,
mushroom cloud,
10 miles high.
12 miles clear before
shock wave hits,
no damage sustained to our ship.
Fire visible over wide area,
mission accomplished!
Let's head home, boys."

"I've never seen anything like that before, and I don't want to see it ever again." exclaimed one crewman; white faced and shaking.

"What we have unleashed here today has wreaked a terrible vengeance on our enemies. I've flown on incendiary bomb missions all around Japan and what this weapon can do makes them look like fly swatting." agreed another crewman.

He paused and then added, "Here there has been tremendous destruction and immense damage, a terrifying shockwave, and a wave of intense heat that frazzled everything that it touched. We have created a wasteland. Nobody survived that. History will bear witness to this day having released a terrible irreversible curse on all the citizens of our world."

A third man spoke, "This has been nothing short of a necessary evil that we have been forced to inflict on the enemy in order to bring a quick end to the war. I sure hope it works, and we never have to do that again."

Captain George Marquardt, the aircraft commander, cut in, "Boys, we in Crew B-10 are the 'Up An' Atom' team. We had a job to do. It's killing people before they kill us. That is all! No more talking; it's over."

There was silence for a long time as the crew settled back into the long flight home and back to Tinian Island. One hour later I looked back towards Japan and could see a spiralling pall of smoke blackening the skies to the North as Hiroshima, now a totally flattened city, continued to burn furiously. It sickened me, and I floated back into the rear of the plane to contemplate what I had been a witness to. I tried to sleep but was troubled by the same disturbing and alarming words that had been repeated over and over again back in Heaven before this task had begun.

"Oh, fatal day - oh, day of sorrow,
It was no trouble she could borrow;
But in the future she could see
The clouds of infelicity."
He is the bird of ill omen.
How harsh his midnight cry!
It seems to shriek, in mournful sounds,
Death! Death!"

Zebra in t' Chippie
(Written 17th/19th November, 2016)

I were walkin 'ome from t' Orse and 'Ounds;
it were a lovely bright, moonlight night.
I'd only 'ad 6 or 7 pints of best bitter,
and I were feelin quite alright.

I wandered down t' Igh Street,
Swayin' this way and that,
feelin like I didn't ave a care in t' world;
must 'ave looked a right lairy prat.

And then my eyes went out on stalks,
and I couldn't believe what I'd seen.
Across t 'road in t' moonlight,
there it was starin' back at me.

There were a zebra in t' Chippie,
standin' upright bold as brass,
black and white stripes all up his legs,
and disappearin' up his arse.

He stood there so proud and strong,
on those long striped pyjama legs,
'E wasn't doin' out that was wrong,
but 'is snout were in t' pickled eggs.

But t' chippie were closed up for t' night,
and I couldn't go in there to find,
why were a zebra a-standin' there,
mindin' 'is own business mind.

I went 'ome feelin' most perplexed,
you know, I thought I was seein' things,
the sort of hallucinations that,
a night out on t' beer may bring.

Well, nevertheless I slept like a log,
and woke up in t' fire.
In t' mornin' me brain were still a-buzzin',
from what had recently transpired.

A zebra in t' chippie,
I ask yer 'ow can that be right;
it's not the sort of thing yer expect to see,
on a lovely moonlit night.

So when the lunchtime came around next day,
I'd 'ave chips and a wing of skate,
down in t' chippie that afternoon,
before the hour got too late.

I resolved to solve my riddle there and then;
there were questions I needed to answer.
why in the world were there a zebra in t' chippie,
munchin' away on the pickled eggs, the stripy legged prancer.

The sign outside t' chippie said fish and chips;
It were clear what the man were sellin';
I stood outside with me mouth salivatin'
from the aromas I was smellin'.

Then I went inside and joined t' queue,
as we shuffled towards t' till,
and then I asked to see the boss.
I think 'is name were Bill.

'E came out front in 'is straw 'at,
and greeted me wi' a smile, and said,
"What can I do for thee then lad?"
in his confident fishmonger style.

"Eee! I just wanted to know something;
I've a question that's mighty queer;
I walked past 'ere late last night,
and there was a zebra standin' 'ere."

Now Bill he pulled me quietly aside,
and said, "Aye lad, there is good reason,
you see fish stocks are dwindlin' fast on t' Dogger Bank,
especially in this season.

And I can't see it improvin' soon,
what wi' stingy EU quotas,
our fishin' industry's all but dead,
killed by bureaucratic Brussels voters.

The Russians send their factory ships;
the French and Spanish steal the rest,
while we scrape along doin' nothing' wrong,
still tryin' t' do our level best."

"So although I know it says 'Fish and Chips'
on t' sign above the door,
I'm afraid to say that the time 'as come,
that we're sellin' fish no more.

You see, lad, we've 'ad to diversify,
or take t' business to t' wall;
we've got 'ungry customers t' satisfy;
they still want their hot grub and all.

So I've been out on t' safari in Africa,
on t' Serengeti plains in t' sizzlin' 'eat,
and made a deal with tribesman there
to supply me wi' fresh meat."

"That zebra that yer saw last night,
'as been t' t' butcher's 'ook;
'E's in t' back all ground to mince;
I'll show thee if yer want to 'ave a look.

I'm puttin' 'im on as t' special this week;
I'm doin' stripy sausages and burgers yer see,
and you could say they're sellin' like 'ot cakes,
would you want one for yer tea?

"Well, no," I said, "I came 'ere for skate and chips."
Again I were feelin' quite vexed.
"OK!" he said, "Come back next week,
we're tryin' out wildebeest patties next."

Chelmsford 2012 - Many Hearts - One Mind
A novel by Michael Haley
ISBN 978-1-910104-76-7

Chelmsford 2012 - Many Hearts - One Mind
is the 1st novel in a 2 part series

In 2012 the Olympics came to London.
After 2 dry winter's the government declared a drought.
Soon after, it started raining and didn't stop for 4 months.
The Queen celebrated her Diamond Jubilee.
Chelmsford was granted city status.
And became the First City of Essex.

Tiny was running a small computer games company.
He planned to transform his baby into a global player.
Work colleague, Hugh, was Tiny's oldest, funniest and fattest friend.
He was eating, drinking, and joking himself into oblivion.
Norman was the company's young computer games genius.
He had been totting up notches on the bedpost.
Gordon was the company accountant.
He was a gay activist with his own agenda.

The story up to July 2012 changed all their lives.

First City of Essex - Many Diversions One Destination
Written by Michael Haley
ISBN 978-1-910530-04-7

First City of Essex - Many Diversions, One Destination
Is the 2nd novel in a 2 part series

2012 was a momentous year for Britain, and for Chelmsford.
The year began with a drought, and then it didn't stop raining for 4 months.
Chelmsford was granted city status
and became the First City of Essex.
The Queen celebrated her Diamond Jubilee.
Then there was the Olympics, and the Paralympics.

Will Tiny's grandiose plans for 1stCitySoft succeed?
Will Hugh live to enjoy the fruits of his labours?
Will Norman and Clarisa stay together?
What will happen to Gordon, the crooked accountant?
Will the Vicarage Road gay clique survive?
Is there a future for Duncan and Caroline?
Will 2012 be a special year for the mighty Clarets?
Will the World come to an end on 21st December?

The story up to December 2012 changed all their lives.

An Idea Appeared
A collection of Poems and Songs by Michael Haley
ISBN 978-1-910330-64-1

I'd been writing poems and songs since I was a spotty teenager, and stories perhaps since I was a wrinkly pensioner. Therefore I decided to attempt to compile and edit all of my writings of any quality from the very beginning up to the present day.

Like many of my writing projects, this seemed to grow exponentially, until it occurred to me that the editing and compiling into an acceptable format, was going to take many months of hard work. So in the interim I put together this little collection of poems and songs, illustrating the full range of my creations.

That is how the little poetry compilation "An Idea Appeared" came about.

Perhaps the little collection could be regarded as an aperitif, or an hors d'oeuvres, or even an amuse bouche, but then again it's none of them because there aren't any French songs or poems included. Whatever the classification, I hope you enjoy this little sampler, and come back for more.

An idea appeared
Written 13th September, 1999

When pen came to paper an idea appeared;
at first just a verse, or a phrase that endeared;
Some words in a row that sounded quite clever,
Complementing each other by standing together;
Some lines once refined and a rhyme neatly timed;
a discreet little meter, a sing-song like chime,
Then an idea that swelled, blossomed, evolved,
until all the loose ends were tried, tied, and solved,
and every fine detail was tested and cleared;
When pen came to paper, an idea appeared.

Turning Over Stones
A compilation of poems, songs, stories and recording history of Michael Haley covering the period 1949 to 1998
ISBN: 978-1-911044-46-8

I have been assembling a complete collection of my writings over a long period of time, and when the project seemed to grow exponentially I decided to convert the project into 3 separate undertakings.

This is Volume 1 - a collection titled "Turning Over Stones" covering the period from 1949 to 1998.
The title comes from a song which I wrote the lyric for in July, 1998. But it also serves to illustrate the process I have been going through to uncover (hopefully) all my gems.

Each individual creation is preceded by a short descriptive text adding further to the understanding of moods, feelings and attitudes at the time of writing.
It is a fascinating and highly personal insight into one man's life.

Volume 2 will be "Tall Words on a Wall" covering the
period from 1998 to 2004,
to be published sometime in the future.
This title derives from the final song lyric of this compilation which was written in June, 2004.

Volume 3 will be "Walls Come Tumbling Down" covering the
period 2004 to the present day.
This will also be published in the future.
The title just seems at this moment in time to be an appropriate one for what happened in the world and in my life since 2004.

All 3 volumes bring together a collection of written work including biographical extracts, poems, song lyrics, a recording history, and other pieces of writing. The items are assembled in a chronological order to illustrate my life and times working with words beginning in 1949 and finishing in the present day.

Maybe this collection is a biography or maybe it's a chronology.
Maybe it's a bit of both?
There is a lot more to come in the other 2 volumes.

Angel's Rainbow
Written by Michael Haley
ISBN 978-1-912192-44-1

Angel's Rainbow

It's about Life and Death
It's about Heaven and Earth
It's about Time and Space
It's about Truth and Faith
It's about Tragedy and Salvation
It's about Reality and Magic
It's about the Beginning and the End
It's about History and the Here and Now
It's about the Past, the Present, and the Future
It's about Ordinary people and Famous people
It's about Rights and Wrongs
It's about You and Me
It's about Angels
It's not about Religion

Michael Hartson is a senior partner in a City of London company called Connor, Hartson and Bromberger Futures. By chance, he manages to avoid being a victim in a major terrorist incident, and consequently he encounters an old tramp in the park. Later, he finds that the tramp, called George O'Donnell, has not only given him some life-changing advice, but has also sneaked a talisman, in shape of a small purple velvet six-pointed star, into his wallet. From that moment on, Michael's life begins to take a new course.

Tragically, he dies only six months later. Only then does he begin to learn just how important the little velvet star will become.

Michael finds himself involved in a long and difficult quest to earn the Angel's Rainbow.

As the story unfolds, through a series of real life, historically significant, world shattering incidents, he asks many questions and learns many valuable lessons, while earning a series of coloured stars that combine to complete the Angel's Rainbow.

Lightning Source UK Ltd.
Milton Keynes UK
UKHW012311150819
348039UK00002B/189/P